# The World Elsewhere

## and Other Stories

## by Nirmal Verma

readers international

English translations © Oxford University Press, Delhi 1986

First published outside South Asia by Readers International, by arrangement with Oxford University Press for sale outside South Asia 1988

Printed and bound in Great Britain by Richard Clay Ltd, Bungay, Suffolk

ISBN 0-930523-46-6

# Contents

# Under Cover of Darkness

Bano had to cut across three goat-paths to reach our house. 'Any news?' She always fired the question at me immediately on entering the room. I was sorely tempted to lie to her and say, 'Yes, there is. It's all settled. We'll be leaving for Delhi soon.' But I desisted. Bano was too shrewd not to see through my lies. Instead, I lay silently, with my eyes closed.

As usual, she came over and felt my forehead. When her touch was cold I knew that my fever had not gone down. But when it was warm I felt elated. Eagerly opening my eyes I would ask, 'Bano, don't you think I am getting better?' Looking disappointed she would reply hopefully, 'But your temperature is bound to shoot up in the evening!' She was unhappy every time my temperature came down. She knew that as long as my fever lasted I could not leave her and would stay put in Simla. Sometimes when I heard her footsteps I quickly applied a wet towel to my forehead. 'Feel my forehead.' I would reach out for her hand and brush it against my brow. 'Cold, is it?' Without a word, Bano would start looking out of the window.

Outside one could see the forests enveloped in a blue haze, and lofty mountains, range upon range.

When the curtain fluttered in the breeze the room was drenched with a dream-like fragrance, wafted from afar.

'Beyond those mountains lies Delhi. You know that, of course', I said.

Bano nodded. She had no interest in Delhi, had never been to that city. Her father's office remained in Simla all year round. I pitied her.

'I have been to our house', she said, changing the subject.

The mention of 'our house', which on other days swept me off my feet, today held no interest for me.

'Bano, you can keep my share of plums', I said, without opening my eyes.

'Who cares about eating your rotten plums!' Bano said, peeved. 'Take them along when you go to Delhi—your precious cargo of rotten plums!' She went into the verandah.

It made me angry. But when one is ill, one cannot work oneself up to a high pitch of anger. In illness all feelings peter out without reaching the crescendo of passion. If one cries no tears come—only the eyelids flutter. If one feels exhilarated the heart does not beat faster—only the lips tremble.

The house which Bano had referred to as 'our house' was said to be haunted and lay deserted all year. They said an English woman had committed suicide in this house. In one of the bathrooms we used to store our treasure trove of raw plums and apricots. It was a closely guarded secret and no one was aware of our goings on.

Bano kept swinging in the verandah a long time. As the swing went up, her *salwar* puffed out like a balloon. The rhythmic creaking of the swing acted like a soporific; I dozed off and had dreams. I always remembered the dreams I had in the afternoons. I dreamed that the *chaprasi* had come from the office to fetch father's lunch. He laughed and told us that we would soon move down to Delhi. Then I saw Bano throwing apricots out of the window of the haunted house. Far away in the hills I could see the English-woman who had committed suicide leaning out of the window of the Kalka-Simla train. With out-stretched hands she grabbed at the apricots which Bano cast to the winds.

When I woke Bano had been gone a long time.

In the evening when mother brought in the tea I asked her if the *chaprasi* had come in the afternoon.

'Yes, he did. Why?'

'Did he tell you anything?'

'No, nothing. What's the matter with you?'

I kept silent. Propping myself up against the pillow I sipped my tea.

After some time mother took my temperature and im-mediately after jerked down the column of mercury. Earlier I used to insist on knowing my temperature. But she was reluctant to tell the truth and I stopped asking. I tried to guess it by watching the expres-sion on her face. Sometimes when I became grave she would say, 'Now get well, and then we shall leave for Delhi.' She said it in a casual manner, as if it was entirely up to me to get well or remain ill; as if I was keeping ill out of sheer cussedness and had to be cajoled into getting well. This would put me into a temper and turning aside I would lie facing the window. For a long time she would not realize that I was angry, till I stiffened my legs, clenched my fists, grit my teeth and started breathing heavily. Mother, who would all this while have been looking out of the window, would get alarmed. She would look at me intently, sigh, and sit down on the bed, by my side. I sensed at once that she had seen through my game, though she never gave me that impression. Taking out a bat of Cadbury's chocolate from the almirah, she would place it under my pillow. 'Don't tell your father about it', she would warn me, running her fingers through my hair. But the very next moment she would forget me; she would be miles away, lost in her own world of thoughts. I knew this from the way her fingers became inert. The piece of chocolate she had given me was not so much to put me in good humour as to keep me out of her way—so that she could again burrow into her shell, undisturbed. I would look at her face without her knowing it. The shadowy lines would be gone and her face would be a blank emptiness. Her eyes would glow with an inner fire and seem to mist over with a thin film. I wanted to delude myself with the pleasant thought that she was thinking of my illness, but in my heart of hearts I knew that her thoughts had nothing to do with me.

I gently put my hand on hers. She started, as if my touch had dragged her back from remote recesses of the mind. She looked hard at me and then kissed me on the lips. I wiped my mouth with my sleeve. She smiled.

'Child, may I ask you something?'

'Yes?'

'If I go away will you be angry?' She looked at me without blinking her eyes.

'Will father go with you?'

'No.'

'Then?' I was puzzled.

She began laughing and lay down by my side.

I put my cheek against hers. Mother was very beautiful and everybody was afraid of her. Sometimes I wondered what it was about her that kept everyone on their toes. I was also afraid of her, though—specially of her eyes when she looked at me closely.

A long time back I once accompanied father to his friend's house. Our path lay along a ravine and as we climbed up we stopped for a while in the forest grove to regain our breath. The silence of the grove felt eerie.

Now when I looked at mother's eyes I was reminded of that dark forest grove.

Mother's arms were white and smooth as marble. I was shy about touching them. She parted her hair in the middle, sweeping it back tightly, which made her forehead still more prominent. Her ears were small, almost doll-like, and remained hidden under her hair. When she lay by my side I pulled them out from her hair and I was suddenly reminded of what Bano once told me about people with small ears having short lives. I shivered to think of it but I never told mother. I imagined that when she lay dying I would tell her she was dying before her time because of her ears.

Sometimes I had a feeling that she was not particularly worried over my illness, that perhaps there were times she even forgot I was ill. I also knew that mother was not eager to go to Delhi. Once I heard her saying so to Uncle Biren and I wondered why.

For the past few months mother and father had slept in separate rooms. This seemed odd to me. But then there were many mysteries I did not delve into; I simply relegated them to the back of my mind.

Mother's room was at the other end of the gallery and her two windows overlooked mine. Sometimes she could be seen at a window, her bunch of hair like molten gold in the sun. I knew she was sitting by the window, reading.

She had many books scattered all over the place— on the sofa, by the pillow, under the bedstead. Perhaps she slept very little. Often I saw the light burning in her room late into the night.

Once I opened one of her books. On the fly-leaf I saw Uncle Biren's name inscribed in spidery characters in blue ink. It fascinated me. Later I saw his name on many more books which lay about in her room.

This reminded me of Uncle Biren's small cottage which I had visited with mother. One room was choked full with books and there was a step ladder which he used for taking down books from the shelves. The walls of another room were covered with oddly framed paintings before which I would pause for hours. Father told me that Uncle Biren had purchased these paintings in Europe before the War. My feelings for Uncle Biren were a mixture of wonder and pity. How could he bring himself to live in this lonely cottage all by himself, the year through, winter and summer?

Among father's friends Uncle Biren had a distinct standing, for it was only he that father invited to take tea in my room—others he received in the drawing room. When Uncle Biren came I was not packed off at bedtime. I was allowed to stay on while they sat talking long hours. They were pleasant evenings.

One evening when Uncle Biren called on us he was so funnily dressed that for a moment I did not recognize him. Long boots which came up to his knees, a khaki knapsack slung over one shoulder and a camera over the other, a sola hat, and quaintest of all a goatee which did not suit his face. His pockets bulged with books.

He came to my bed and shook hands with me. Uncle Biren was always like that. He always greeted me as one greets a normal, healthy person: and he never wasted his breath enquiring after my health.

Mother sat beside us, busy knitting. She cast a fleeting glance at Uncle Biren and lowered her head. Uncle Biren told us that he was bound for Kufri. He would stay the night in the Rest House and return the following evening. 'I am told the watchman of the Rest House has been living in Kufri for the last thirty years', Uncle Biren said. 'He must know a lot about Kufri.'

A faint smile spread on mother's face. 'You have been at this game for more years than one can remember', she said without looking up.

'Oh, so you don't believe me. Then you must look at my Notes.' Uncle Biren's blue eyes lit up. Somehow any mention of his 'book', 'A History of Simla', always made mother smile.

'Sometimes I come across valuable scraps of information while collecting material for my book', Uncle Biren said.

'What kind of information, Uncle?' I asked.

I always showed keen interest in Uncle's book. It buoyed up his spirits.

'Once I chanced upon an old photograph', Uncle Biren said. 'An Englishman must have taken it.'

'A photograph of . . .?' mother asked, looking up from her knitting.

'Of a crowd at a race course. Most of the faces were indistinct. But one face, a girl's, had come out clearly. She was standing by the pavilion, an umbrella in her hand. Everyone's eyes were glued to the running horses but her's seemed to be held by something behind her. A rather incongruous note. Her looking back like this.' Uncle Biren suddenly stopped. The knitting lay quiet in mother's hands.

'The caption under the photograph read: "Annandale, Simla—1903". Fifty years ago. And she was still looking back, umbrella in hand.'

Uncle Biren laughed, as if at his own whimsy. Mother looked up at him, her eyes icy. Sometimes I wondered why Uncle Biren indulged in such meaningless talk.

'At times I feel it is much easier to write about men than about cities', Uncle Biren said. 'I've assembled a huge mass of notes, old photographs, travelogues on Simla, but I doubt I will ever succeed in writing my book.'

'Why?' mother asked.

'Because . . . because every city is so much absorbed in itself. It does not let you pry into its secrets easily.' Uncle Biren got up. He touched my forehead.

'I met the doctor while coming down', he said, bending over me. 'He said you will be fit enough to walk about in a few days' time.'

'Will you sit up a moment?' he said, taking the camera

from his shoulder. 'I'll take your photograph. Let's see how you look.'

After taking my photograph he picked up his walking stick, ready to leave.

'When will you come again?' mother asked, looking him straight in the eye for the first time.

'Perhaps tomorrow evening—I'll drop in for a minute.' When Uncle looked at mother his eyes became dazzled and he turned his face.

'Uncle Biren . . .', I said shyly.

'Yes, child?'

'I'll take a photograph.'

He smiled and handed me the camera.

I looked at mother.

'No, no, not me, son', she said, her words tumbling over each other.

'You will not be alone. Uncle Biren will also be in it.' Uncle Biren turned pale and cast a fleeting look at mother. She rose from her chair without any more fuss, saying to me, 'You are very wilful.'

'Uncle Biren, you stand by the railing—in the sun. And mother you stand to the right.' I climbed out of the bed and stood leaning the wall. My head reeled. But the photograph was a great success. I have it with me to this day.

I did not know when darkness crept into the room. Uncle Biren had been gone a long time. Only mother was there, reclining in a chair by my side, silent and motionless. I did not ask for the light. I like the feeling of darkness slowly invading a room.

Suddenly the memory of a particular evening flitted across my mind. This was much before I fell ill. Mother had taken me to Uncle Biren's house.

Uncle Biren was taken aback on seeing us. He let us in at the wicket gate, looking flustered.

'Pono, you here?' It was the first time I heard Uncle Biren addressing mother by her name. Coming from his lips her name rang strangely. Mother started laughing. I can't say why, but I didn't like the way she laughed. I felt cramped and a vague numbness spread over my heart.

'We came out for a stroll', mother said. 'We thought we might as well say hello to you.' It was the first time I'd heard mother lying.

For a fleeting second Uncle Biren's blue eyes clouded with doubt; then he held my finger and led us into his cottage.

I saw his library for the first time. He showed me photographs of the mountain peaks of Simla, its valleys and waterfalls. He had collected these for his projected book. A lamp with a light-green shade rested on the table by the side of a heap of books. He brought out two slabs of chocolate from somewhere. I was not prepared for this sleight of hand and he laughed at my discomfiture. 'I have laid by quite a stock of chocolates', he said. 'It comes in handy during the winter when I'm snowed in.' I looked at Uncle Biren. How different from father! He had none of that oppressive grimness and tenseness which I associated with father. There was an intangible tenderness about Uncle Biren. Above his trim beard the soft eloquence of his eyes seemed to shed the coarseness from everything they ranged over.

'Have you ever seen a snow-capped peak from close range?' he asked me. I shook my head.

'The snow looks blue', he said. 'I took a colour photograph. . .' He went into the adjoining room.

Idly I thumbed through his albums which were lying on a table. Each photograph represented a view of Simla: Glenn, Jakhu, Chetwick Falls. I easily recognized each of these spots. Uncle had not shown up and I began to fell bored. I picked up another album, a small one, which was lying at the corner of a bookshelf. I turned the first page and a known face stared at me. It was a picture of mother.

Was mother ever like this? My heart missed a beat: it was the same broad forehead but it had the small red *bindi* which mother no longer puts on. Two locks of hair fell over her shoulders. She was wearing a full-sleeved sweater and her small ears were hidden under her hair, the same as now. Looking at her expression I had a sudden feeling that that face had nothing to do with me or with father. It was mother, but I could not see my mother in her.

Hearing Uncle Biren's footsteps I guiltily put away the album.

When we came out onto the lawn the shadows of the evening had begun to fall. Wrapped in a shawl, mother was sitting on a stone bench. Uncle Biren sat on the grass near mother's feet. 'Where were you all this while?' She tenderly pulled me to her. I looked searchingly into her face. The same eyes, mouth and forehead: separately they closely resembled her features in the photograph but together the impression was different in a way I could not define. Perhaps it was an expression which annihilated distance and yet never came closer.

'What's the matter, son?' Mother ran her fingers through my bedraggled hair. I shrank into myself and looked away.

Mother did not pay me any further attention. We

sat quietly, lost in our own thoughts. Since our coming  Uncle Biren had not talked to mother. It seemed
strange but its meaning was lost on me.

A blue haze had descended upon the lawn. Among
the distant hills lights shone like glow-worms; the
outlines of the hills having been blurred by darkness,
the sky seemed to nestle closer to the earth.

While I was ill I often recalled this evening,
although nothing unusual had happened to distinguish it from other evenings. Uncle Biren accompanied us some distance home and when mother assured
him we would manage all right he turned back.
Swiftly, I had gone ahead. I stopped and looked back.
Mother was not there. I retraced my steps, peering
into the darkness, my heart beating faster.

At the turn of the road I found mother leaning over
the railing, the end of her sari fluttering in the breeze.
She was looking below at Uncle Biren's cottage. In
the evening it looked lonely and deserted. A pale
streak of light from the library window lay across the
lawn.

For a while we stood silent and then mother resumed her walk. Her gait was so slow that she
seemed to be walking in her sleep. When she came up
to me she stared at me for a long time with helpless
eyes. Then she drew me close and put her cold, dry
lips to my mouth.

After some days I felt the taste of illness begin to leave
my mouth and life seemed to surge back slowly into
my limbs. I had the windows opened and the curtains
drawn so that I could bathe in the soft furry warmth
of the sunlight.

One morning I came out onto the verandah. A little away from me, auntie was busy hanging out her washing on the wooden railing. Stealthily, I crept past her and stepped into the balcony at the back of father's room. The doors and windows of the room at the other end were barred and no curtains were hanging in them. When mother went away to her aunt's, father would lock up her room, carry all his things upstairs into the study and spend his nights there.

The balcony looked forlorn. In front of me in the walled compound of the school I could see small boys, satchels in hand, standing four in a row, reciting their prayers in a nasal sing-song: 'God's name comes to my lips with the fervour of a keen desire.' Unable to stand their lacerating voices any more, I looked beyond, over the haunted house across the ravine, and then along the serpentine path which lost itself behind the compound of Bano's house. Fetching father's old discarded walking-stick, at the end of which I had tied a red piece of cloth, I waved it above my head. This was a favourite game with me and Bano. She saw me and waved back. Then she pointed me to her mother, who also waved. Embarrassed, I threw away the stick and ran inside.

Before I could enter my room a servant came to tell me that father wanted to see me. A wave of joy surged through me. It was rare for father to invite me to his room. Hastily, I bit my nails to make sure that they were clean; father always looked at my nails the first thing.

Father's room had a distinct individuality compounded of the smell of cigar smoke, an oppressive

stillness, subdued lighting which did not change
night or day; above it all a sour medicinal odour hung
pervasively in the air, like a layer of thinly spun colour.

'What were you doing outside?' I knew father's
moods. There was no anger in his voice.

'I was looking for Bano.' I fumbled and became silent. 'Father!'

Father looked up.

'I am well now. The fever has left me.'

Father placed my hands one upon the other and
held them in his big hairy hands. 'You must rest in
bed a few days more', he said.

'Father, when are we going to Delhi?' It was a
question I always asked whenever I met him.

Father looked so forlorn. The stillness that reigned
in his room seemed to permeate the whole house.
Without mother every room looked empty and desolate.

Mother had left for her aunt's place without seeing
me. I happened to wake in the middle of the night before she went.

My room was dark. In the breeze the window curtain flew up and kept fluttering over my pillow. For
some time a doubt hovered in my mind; everything
in the room seemed to have shifted from its proper
place: the window on my left had quietly moved
down to the middle of the wall, the door had slipped
two yards to the right. The door was ajar and from
father's room showed a thin mercurial column of
light so slender and fragile that a touch would have
shivered it to bits. Suddenly the door, flapping like a

black birdwing, stood open for a second, then slowly closed. As it closed a beam of light streaked across the floor and climbed the opposite wall. I heard someone breathing heavily behind the door and I thought it was mother come to fasten the latch. But no one came. I heard voices, now coming from afar; indistinct, wordless sounds. Then, so close it was, as if someone were whispering into my ear:

'No, you won't go in.' It was father.

A thin cry, like a bright sliver of glass, pierced the heart of darkness. What was wrong with mother? Why did she shriek in this strange manner?

'Let go my hand!' she cried.

'Pono, I won't allow you to go in.'

'Who are you to stop me? Aren't you ashamed of yourself?'

'Pono, don't shout, he's sleeping.'

'I won't shout. Let me go in.'

'No, no, not now.'

'Do you think I am mad? Do you think I'll tell him . . .?'

'Pono, go to your room. You are not in your senses.'

Before father could say more the curtain parted and my bed was flooded with light. I saw two marble-like arms spread against the curtain and a shadowy figure with two hungry and distraught eyes. Thin, long fingers clutched the curtain, trembling violently, and a nose piece shone like a start above quivering lips. I glimpsed the phantasmagoric sight in the fleeting instant before the curtain was pulled across the door. Then there were only muffled groans.

After this I could not believe my ears. Slow continuous laughter behind the curtain. No, it could not be mother. I had never before heard her laughing like that. I could neither hear nor see anything more. My mind went blank and I felt that the darkness had gathered itself into something tangible, something foul and ragged that coiled and twisted before my eyes.

I was lying on the terrace one afternoon during my convalescence when no one took any notice of me and I had my way with everything. Father did not drop into my room in the evenings and I had not seen Uncle Biren for a long time. If any one was sorry about my recovery it was Bano. Had I remained ill the chances of our going to Delhi would have receded.

Behind the terrace there were two low hills, pointing towards the sky like a pair of scissors. Between them a forest range stretched far into the distance. When the train bound for Kalka passed through it, a column of smoke drifted above the trees towards the sky.

'Bano, we'll be leaving for Delhi soon', I told Bano, who was busy picking apricots from the terrace. Her skirt was filled with apricots. She knelt and her booty spilt on the ground.

'Here, eat this', she said, picking up a yellow-ripe apricot. 'It's nice.'

I shook my head. Father had forbidden me to eat apricots.

'Its ripe, it will do you no harm', she said, and without waiting for my answer popped it into her mouth. She turned the apricot in her cheek and said that if it was turned often enough the saliva made the fruit more juicy.

'So it is settled that you are going to Delhi', she said, sucking noisily at the apricot.

'Yes, as soon as mother returns.'

'Where has your mother gone?'

'To her aunt's place.'

'Are you sure?' Bano looked at me mysteriously.

'What's the matter, Bano?' I asked, puzzled.

'Nothing. Just asking.' She pressed the apricot between her lips and added, 'I won't tell you. Mother has warned me not to.'

I felt angry but smiled, feigning indifference. When I was angry I tried to hide my feelings behind a smile so that no one would think me an ill-tempered fool.

The hills behind the terrace were grey under the lowering clouds and their thin elongated shadows flitted across them from the east.

'Is Delhi beyond those mountains?' Bano asked me.

'Delhi is in the plains', I replied. 'One has to climb over those hills to reach Delhi.'

Bano looked at me sceptically. 'But below us is the Annandale Race Course, and beyond that the ravine. Is Delhi in the ravine?'

Without trying to satisfy her curiosity I turned my back on her.

Near the terrace was the pavilion and behind the pavilion the guest room of the haunted house. Bano threw the apricot stones into the guest room and stood leaning against the wall.

All Simla was hushed in the afternoon; only the sound of falling apricots punctuated the silence. Bano beckoned me to her. The glass of one of the guest house doors was broken. She peeped through the hole and invited me to join her.

The room was empty, its wallpaper faded. It was full of stale air and cobwebs. In the middle of the floor there was a small circle of light which seemed to change from white to faded yellow and back again. In the darkness the spot of light looked eerie.

'That English woman must have lived in this room', Bano whispered.

'And she must have died in this room', I added, and a shiver ran down my spine. I saw a face gradually emerging on the peeled-off plaster of the wall. Its mouth gaped and its lustreless eyes seemed to mock me, and I heard laughter. It must have been the face of the woman who had taken her own life here, years ago . . . her laughter reminded me of mother's laughter that night.

'Bano, did your mother tell you something about my mother?'

'How does that concern you?'

The doors of the deserted house rattled in the wind.

'Bano, when I was ill, sometimes I had strange feelings. I felt I was just like mother—that there was something common between us. Something which no one lies about. I saw an apparition wrapped in snow, whose hands were white as marble and always remained dangling in the air. An apparition which coming from behind suddenly bottled me up—and then I fell apart from my own self. Yes, from my own being, Bano!'

Bano shook like a leaf and her eyes grew wide with fear.

We were all packed and ready to leave. Labels had
been pasted on all the boxes, bags and bed-rolls—
'Simla–Delhi', and father's name in bold letters below. The servants and peons from father's office ran
all over the place, busy with the arrangements; the
house bustled with activity.

Mother was in her room upstairs, doing nothing.
Father had asked me not to go to her; perhaps she was
not well. I hadn't met her since she returned from her
aunt's place. She had arrived at night when I was
asleep.

Having nothing to do, I knocked about the house
till I felt suffocated with boredom. Keeping out of the
way, I escaped from the house.

Descending the footpath I started along the ravine,
picking pine cones till both my pockets were stuffed
with them. On the distant hills the late sunlight still
lingered, too tired to merge with darkness.

I had come a long way from home and when I
started walking back I suddenly spotted Uncle
Biren's tiny cottage, down below, cosily ensconced
in a cluster of trees. I remembered that particular
evening when I had come to the cottage with mother.
Ever since mother had gone to stay with her aunt
Uncle Biren had stopped calling on us. Once I had
asked father about Uncle Biren. But his expression had
become so hard that I dared not pursue the subject.

I walked down to the cottage. In the westering sun
the sloping roof was a glowing red. The wicket gate
was open. I tiptoed on to the lawn. The wind sighing
through the grass deepened the sense of desolation.
At the edge of the lawn I could see the stone bench on
which mother had sat.

I gently knocked at the door, 'Uncle Biren, Uncle.'
My voice went ringing through that lonely, mute
cottage. I felt it was not my own voice but an unfamiliar one which chased my own.

'Come in. The door is open.'

I went in. The dim light of the table-lamp fell on
the books and the papers which lay in disorder on the
table. Uncle Biren asked me to sit on his bed and pulled up his easy chair beside me.

'Have you walked alone, this long distance?' He
took my hand in his and smiled.

Suddenly his eyes fell upon my bulging pocket and
I went red in the face.

'What have you in those pockets of yours?' he
asked me. 'Pine cones?'

I nodded.

'What will you do with them?'

'They are for the train.'

'For the train?' Uncle Biren's face became a question mark.

'Yes, we are leaving for Delhi tonight, Uncle.'

He looked at me without blinking. Then he got up
and without taking further notice of me started gazing out of the window. A suffocating silence filled the
room. I felt he had known about our going away.
When he turned from the window his blue eyes
shone.

'You remember the photograph you took that
day?' he asked me. 'Its ready. Would you like to see
it?'

He took out an envelope from the almirah and
handed it to me. 'You are quite an expert', he said.
'The photograph has come out very well.'

I looked at the photograph. The vent, which I had consigned to limbo, returned vividly.

Against a hazy backdrop of mountains I saw Uncle Biren standing close to the railing of the balcony, his arm unknowingly touching mother's sari. And mother . . . she stood with half-closed eyes, her lips parted, as though she was on the point of uttering something and had then abruptly checked herself.

I kept looking at the photograph for some time.

Then I was reminded of the train journey which I had to make. I climbed off the bed. 'Well, Uncle . . .'. I was too overwhelmed to unburden my thoughts.

Uncle Biren came close to me. He touched my hair and gently kissed me on the forehead, the same way mother had kissed me that night.

We came out.

'May I see you home?' he asked me.

I shook my head. I knew the way. For a while we stood silent in the verandah.

'Son . . .'. Startled I looked at him.

'Your mother once wanted a book. I forgot about it . . .'. He hesitated.

'Please give it to me. I'll take it with me.'

While handing me the book I thought he wanted to say something but could not.

The cottage was left behind. I made my way back along the deserted road. When I neared home I stopped under a lamp-post and examined the book.

The envelope containing the photograph was lying within its pages.

The book was very old. Even today I can vividly recall its yellow and brittle pages: *Flaubert's Letters to*

*George Sand*. Those days I was not familiar with the names of Flaubert or George Sand. Years after, when I read the book, mother was no more and Uncle Biren had long since left the country and settled in Italy.

But that day the book had no significance for me. For a long time I stood under the lamp-post, holding the book and looking at the room upstairs.

The window of mother's room was closed, but a sepulchral light shone through.

That was our last evening in Simla.

*Translated by Jai Ratan*

# The Dead and the Dying

He opened the bedding and unrolled it on the floor. The floor was quite warm although the rooms cooled down at night. There was no breeze that night, only a clean bright darkness and he felt he would fall asleep at once. But this was hope, not desire. During the past few nights he had lost his sleep. This had left him indifferent and his anxiety of the first couple of days seemed quite ridiculous now.

He got up, watchful. The night nurse had come to the door and stopped in passing.

'How is your patient now?' she asked. There was a vague solicitude in her voice, but without intimacy, so that it appeared somehow naked. At first he had found it queer, this reference to 'his patient', as though he were a kind of guard. But now these were mere words he heard and disposed of every night.

'Why, what's the matter—are you asleep?' the nurse asked a little testily.

'No, but speak a little softly. *He* is asleep.'

This was not a rebuke but an effort to fill a blank. The effort failed because the nurse was now annoyed. Not in the manner of a nurse, but of a woman—offended.

'Did he urinate?'

He hesitated a little, and then nodded his head.

'If he did, where is it?'

The bottle was empty, propped up on the stool like a witness.

'You haven't thrown it away, have you?'

'No—he did it in the bed.'

'The bed?' The nurse threw him an exasperated glance as though he—not the man in bed—were the patient.

'Will you be sleeping here?'

'Yes.'

'This time when he wants to do it, call me, I'll make him do it in the bottle.'

When the nurse started to leave, he followed her to the door. Panic gripped him. To spend the entire night alone with the patient seemed suddenly impossible. At the door he hesitated. There was the bare corridor of the hospital outside, smouldering after the day's heat. It was pointless walking out. He turned back.

At first, in the early days, he wouldn't have turned back. Every time a doctor or a nurse came along on their rounds he would attach himself to them. He would want to ask everything all over again. Instead of the words, he would listen to the intonation of the voices and draw his own inferences. They would walk away embarrassed, trying to avoid him. He would pursue them, right until they entered another ward. It seemed absurd, when he thought about it later, that he should indulge in these antics, this man going on forty—an educated, respectable-looking man at that, hovering around the doctors like a jittery female. Now they hardly paid him any attention.

He turned back and a faint delusion shot through him like a beam of light. Their room, a little cubicle, was wedged between two wards. Groans mounted in waves from both sides and broke against the walls. When he wasn't able to sleep he would listen to the waves rising from those agonized bodies, and then he had this illusion . . . the hospital was a large ship battling with the waves while he and his patient lay safely inside, tucked away in a cabin.

The old man lying on the bed turned over. His eyes were open, like yellow blobs of cotton-wool, and a little below a gaping hole where the mouth had been.

At once he came to himself, breaking off the fantasy. Going over to the bed he bent over the pillow.

'Do you need anything?'

He watched the patient intently. The breathing rose in quick succession and then declined, drier than ever. He is off somewhere, he thought, and decided to accompany him. But then the old man decided to stop and his dim eyes returned from the wilderness. He riveted them on him.

You want something?' Every question was a mindless chant. Sometimes it drew out a reply, at other times it came back, empty.

'Won't you sleep?' The old man opened his mouth.

'I'll sleep. Can I get you anything?'

'Will you sleep on the floor?'

'I always sleep on the floor. Or have you forgotten!'

He tried to melt his anger into irony. It remained neither this nor that, it just spread out and smudged.

They had a two-bed private ward. One bed stood

vacant. No patient had been assigned to it so far. It seemed they were not as eager to bring in a new patient as to be rid of the old one. Let them wait, he would say to himself. How long will they hold out.

'You will sleep on the floor', the old man said. After every trip be returned to the old mark.

'Don't fret for me', he said. 'I'm quite comfortable.'

'I know that', the old man said.

'What do you know?' he asked sharply. But without raising his voice—he kept note of that. He had to remind himself time and again, we are not at home, I mustn't fly into a temper. And he felt guilty as well, because every time he raised his voice the old man looked at him, bewildered. A sort of impotence that he had never noticed in him before. He had always been a little afraid of him, not as a child, but later, in the noontime of his life when suddenly his parents became unfamiliar, strangers in the harsh glare.

Now there was no one else. That is why it was terrifying. There was a bare plain where the old man lay—beneath his son's shadow. If he went away the shadow would lift and he would lie there, unprotected. It was uncanny. No matter what he did, *he* would keep lying there, on the bed, quietly, holding his breath. The first time the nurse had pulled down his pyjamas for an injection it had been unbearable. That he should be allowed to stand there and look at the white shrunken thighs. Nor did he take away his gaze. He stood there, hypnotised, looking at his exposed limbs.

Both kept lying there, the one on the bed, the other on the floor.

'How many days leave do you have?' the voice from the bed asked.

'Ten days.'

'Chhote must have wired you.'

'You mustn't talk too much.'

The old man felt his lips go sour and sticky, but he continued to speak. 'There is nothing certain about me', he said. 'It might take longer than ten days.'

He didn't quite understand, but his heart sank.

'The doctor said—'

'I know what he's said.' The old man cut him short.

He was relieved. He had escaped having to dish up a cheap lie. But he felt apprehensive all the same. The old man knows, he could figure that. How much he knew wasn't clear.

'What are the charges?' the old man suddenly asked.

'What charges?'

'For this room.'

'How does that concern you', he said.

'Why! Doesn't it concern me?' the old man asked in a huff.

'No—I didn't mean that', he stuttered, 'but why should you worry about all that—'

'It's not a question of worrying—at least not any longer.' He slackened. The old man would climb up, then climb down, and though he followed his course up and down he would sometimes slump off on the way, from sheer weariness. At other times he would let go and sit aside, at the edge. His father would scramble about in his private maze and then, when he had quite lost his way, he would take him by the hand and bring him back, here, where he was today, to this bed in the dimly lit cubicle.

The night nurse came in and they both fell silent. The father and son liked this nurse. Unlike the other one she didn't bristle at every word. She was middle-aged but the years had not devoured her. And she had this peculiar kind of assurance which patients sniff from a distance. She came from Kerala. That is why she was so dark, and her clothes looked especially cool for that reason. There was no heat in her, in any case. She spoke to his father in English. That was the reason, perhaps, why he was so pleased with her.

But this time she didn't say anything. Glancing at both of them she smiled. She spread out the crisp white sheets, made a bundle of the soiled ones and threw them under the bed. Then she came up to take his temperature and the old man opened his mouth in an obliging hurry. When she took the thermometer from the mouth he couldn't restrain himself.

'How much is it?'

'That is our worry, not yours', she said. And then she turned to the son. 'And how are you?'

'I'm not a patient!' He tried to joke with her.

'Now you must rest', she said. 'What do you two keep arguing about so late into the night?'

There was no reply. He found it curious that a stranger should think their conversations an argument. It was embarrassing too, and he looked at her glumly.

On her way out she stopped at the threshold and signed to him to come out.

'I—' she hesitated, weighing her words against his

stark gaze. 'I spoke to the doctor', she said in a hushed voice.

'Yes?' he said.

'Don't let him guess—It's no use.'

'Yes', he said.

'If you'd like to, come and have tea with us at about 11 o'clock. But if you go to sleep I shan't come and wake you.' She smiled again and then crossed the corridor with a quick step and went into the staff room.

With a sigh of relief he sat down on the bench in the corridor. The old man would go to sleep soon. Hopefully. He wanted to go in and fetch his cigarettes. His mouth had gone dry. But instead of getting up he stretched out on the bench. His patient was not asleep. When he did go to sleep he could make out at once—by his breathing. Waiting for him to fall asleep he often wondered—does *he* wait as well? In any case both of them stayed awake. The whole business seemed absurd at times and he would think—if I go back to my town, tomorrow, it will make no difference whatever. The brother wired him in panic, thinking they should all be together when the end came. Now they were all together, and together they were waiting for the end—*without* him. You should be ready for anything, the doctors had warned him the very first day. He had tried to prepare himself during these past days, but the person who ought really to have been getting ready kept wandering off. Emptyhanded, he ran after him. Sometimes he forgot that this was his own father. One can't remember relationships twenty-four hours a day.

He stepped into the room. The nurse had switched

off the main light. Only the pink night-light burned in the corner. In its glow everything lost its substance and became spectral—the urine bottle, the phials of medicine, the two tumblers of water—one for him, the other for the old man—and the framed picture of a Delhi monument that he had seen hanging in every room of the hospital.

He smoothed out his bedding on the floor. Before settling down to sleep he flipped through a detective novel. In the pink light the murders in the book seemed inevitable and the corpses went in and out as a matter of course.

The old man wasn't asleep. He watched every movement with an intent stare. At last he blurted out the inevitable question.

'Will you be able to sleep there?'

He was startled. His father always caught him unawares.

'There is a mattress here. I sleep quite well.' He tried to shake him off.

'How well you sleep I know best.'

'What do you know?' His hands hung in mid air

'You simply argue. The habit has never left you.'

'Who is arguing, you or me?' He sat bolt upright now. But his tongue began to wobble. 'You are always nagging me. Do you know how many times you wet your bed while you are asleep?' This he said deliberately, about wetting the bed, to hurt him.

'What are these nurses for, then?' the old man said in a tone of contempt. He had never quite forgotten an officer's manner, although it was an age since he had retired.

'You . . .' he was almost whimpering with rage.

'You think they are your house slaves, do you, that they should go round changing your sheets all night?'

'You are concerned about everyone—yes?' There was a reproach in the old man's voice but it had softened. 'Why don't you sleep at home?' he added.

He looked at the old man and said nothing. This was an hour of peace in the hospital and they were both slowly engulfed by it. It seemed to him that they had come back home. He was walking a little ahead of his father, holding his stick, but his father was nowhere behind. He should have been walking behind, but he was not there. This thought terrified him. He started scrambling over his father's bed.

'What are you doing?' the old man screamed.

'Nothing', he said nervously.

'Don't worry, I havn't pissed yet.' The old man taunted him.

Pissed? No, he was fumbling for something else, pouring with sweat.

As soon as it was daylight he would come and sit outside the room. At the back of the nursing home there was a cluster of low-lying hills, and further on a stretch of dry, barren land. Kites wheeled about over the mounds and rubble, black omens in the white morning glare. He would doze off into a faint sleep— a clean, light sleep that swung over him like a curtain. Indoors the hot water gurgled as it filled the basin. In his absence the old man was scrubbed clean. Sheets soiled with his urine were brought out, dry white sheets taken in. The sweetish odours of soap and detergent sent a tremor as they brushed against him and he would shrink a little into himself. The nurses went

in and he looked at them. Coming out, they glanced
at him. In the midst of this hygenic festivity, the
bright light and cleansing ritual, the nightmares of
the previous night seemed futile. He felt futile himself, for, no matter how helpless the illness, if it be-
longs to another it builds rituals of its own. And it
sweeps off relationships—out of the way, like bits of
rubbish.

His mother and brother were part of this swept
heap.

He would spot them from a distance, coming up to
the gate with hesitant steps. From the distance they
looked like creatures from another world. But as they
crawled up closer he recognized them and went over
hurriedly. Then they would all three sit down, side
by side, silently, in some cool corner of the corridor.

'How has he been?' Mother would ask him. This
was always the first question.

O.K.', he would answer. 'He spent a good night.'

'Did you sleep well?' Brother's voice was always a
little uneasy. He was younger but they addressed
each other with the familiar *tum*. The father's illness,
instead of bringing them closer, had pushed them
apart. He wished that he might take his brother by
the hand, drag him to a lonely corner of some intimate place—in their childhood it had been the kitch-
en—and tell him in complete detail the story of the
long nights he spent with Father. But there was
something that stopped him at the last moment.
There was nothing, really, but he felt obstructed.

'I'll come here straight from the office today. You
go home and rest', his brother said.

'I rest here day and night', he replied.

The brother threw him a covert glance, as though he had attempted a private joke. Every family has its secret signs, and years ago he could catch these in a trice. It was a long time since he had dropped his end of the string.

'Is he conscious throughout?' Mother asked.

'He sleeps most of the time', he said. Whether sleeping is a conscious or unconscious state he had not quite determined.

'He doesn't insist on going home, does he?'

'What home?'

'Our home, whose else?' his mother said irritably.

'He keeps on sleeping', he said. His mother and brother looked at him suspiciously.

'No, don't worry', he said. 'I'm just tired. That's all.'

His words brushed past them. They could sense Babu inside the ward though they could see and hear nothing. At times Mother almost seemed to forget that the patient was once her husband. She peeped in with pitying eyes but couldn't muster enough courage to cross the threshold and face him—the old man, who was hardly able to face anyone any more.

'You go now. I'm here anyway', he said. The brother seemed to be waiting for the signal. At once he got up to leave.

'I will come in the evening', he said consolingly. He was beyond consolation. But he wanted to stop his brother. Don't leave me alone with Babu, we should all remain together, so that we can pull him by the rope, to our side. To our side where there are no nurses, no doctors, no delirious mutterings. Nor those sheets, drenched in urine. On our side, where with a light tap the kitchen door swings open. He used to sit with his mother and brother. Waiting for Babu, in those days, long ago.

He would sit there, clutching at his own side of things and his brother would get up and walk out of the gate.

While leaving, Mother would stop short, as if to stare down those kites wheeling in the sky.

Don't be scared, her eyes seemed to say. Each family has its own separate beginning, they all end the same way.

'You get letters from home?' Mother asked.

'Yes I do. Everything is all right.'

'The children don't miss you, do they?'

He wanted to grab hold of his mother's shoulders and shake her, he wanted them both to go on shaking each other and speaking, like a couple of drunks.

The brother would stop at the gate and call out to her. Startled, she would offer him the bundle. Every day there were the same things—fruit, home-made patties, bread and butter. Some one would whisper in his ears—get along and eat. All day you torture yourself, go and stuff yourself. No one dies with the dying. No one? He would look around him with the guilty eyes of a thief and then he would go and sit on the hospital lawn. Away from the crowd of patients. Spreading his crumpled handkerchief on the green grass he would get the foolish idea that he was on a picnic. That both of them were on a picnic. Babu inside and he outside. Fine! he would think, munching the bread. One needn't go to Okhla or Kutab, its just as good to sit around on the lawn outside the hospital. There isn't any difference at all.

No, it makes no difference to us, whether you sleep on the bed or on the floor, the nurses would assure him. He had begun to recognize them now, although they had all appeared alike in the beginning. Then the ones that came for night duty began to look different from those who came for a few hours in the daytime. Seeing him lying on the floor they would often tell him—you may use the bed, you know. Sleep there if you like. He had no such desire. It was already March and the floor was warm. And he preferred to maintain a distance between the old man and himself by lying there on the floor. That he should snuggle into a bed beside his father's—he couldn't bear that. There had been no such intimacy in their life and he had no inclination to experiment at this late stage.

But the old man's brain kept roving. He looked at the vacant bed with his vacant gaze and couldn't stop the refrain.

'Why, is this meant for a patient?'

'Yes, but nobody will come, don't worry', he would assure him.

'If no one is going to come, why don't you sleep there? Is there any point lying on the floor?'

He would laugh and say, 'But I've told you, these beds are meant for patients, not their relatives.'

'Can you spot those patients' His mouth screwed up in sarcasm. 'Or do you think we must wait to honour them?'

'Here nobody waits for anyone', he said. 'Here there is you and there is me . . . '. He glared at his father. Did he have to cast about for such trivial gains at this late stage?

'You lie on that floor like a martyr, to make a display of your sacrifice', the old man blurted out.

He sprang up, shaking violently.

'Do you realize what you are saying?' His voice quivered. 'I lie on this floor to impress you! Is your mind in order?'

'If my mind was in order I wouldn't have come here to suffer this ill-treatment.'

'You're being ill-treated here, are you? A whole room to yourself, all this expense—'. He swallowed the words.

'O no! I'm very comfortable. What *is* lacking, after all?' There was bitter disdain in the old man's voice.

His blood rushed up. There was a loud hammering in his head. 'You must go on and on, talking nonsense. Do you know what the doctors say about your condition? If we hadn't brought you here by this time you would . . .'.

O Lord! why can't I shut up. I keep arguing. As though *I'm* the sick one. And I should be trying to divert his mind. I should pull him out of this miserable bickering. I should draw him towards things that are real and important. Things one must face in the end.

What sort of real things? He lifted his gaze to the window beyond. There was a grassy patch outside the hospital. Patients from the General Ward came there and strolled about. They looked like prisoners in their blue-striped pyjamas. If his father had stood among them he would be unidentifiable, he thought with a cold shiver. He looked at him lying there—flat like some soiled old rag-doll. Something the children had played with long ago, quite useless now. Not even good enough as a scarecrow. To be afraid of, to frighten others.

He leapt towards the bed in a frenzy and started caressing his body. His father took his hand and put it away. He disliked being touched. Goodness knows how years ago he could ever have slept with Mother. But this time he wouldn't withdraw. With childish obstinacy he again caught hold of his father's hand.

'You keep fretting. Why don't you read something?' he pleaded.

A copy of the Gita lay on the bedside table. At home his father had read it morning and evening. Now, since coming to the hospital, he hadn't touched it.

'In this condition?' The old man gave him a curious look—the bed-pan under him and the Gita in his hands! He laughed soundlessly.

'If you like I'll read it to you.'

The old man said neither yes nor no, he kept staring at the ceiling. His enthusiasm faded. When you hear the Gita or the Ramayana you look into yourself, not like this, gaping at the ceiling. He started reading aloud in a flat tone. The father had scribbled a commentary on the margins of the book in English. He had never trusted anyone else's commentary. While reading he kept glancing at the margin, as though it wasn't a commentary but his father's old diary he was reading furtively.

The old man lifted his hand. He stopped mid-sentence and looked at him nervously.

'What do you think you are doing?' the old man asked.

'Why, I'm reading! Can't you see.'

'Is this the way?'

'What sort of way?'

'To read the Gita, what else? Even schoolboys don't read their Tennyson this way.'

He felt like flinging the book out of the window. But he stopped. The old man's voice had suddenly mellowed. 'When you were little you used to read exactly like this. You are a father now, with two sons of your own, but there isn't a trace of difference in your style of reading.'

He drew a long breath and turned over, as though the little speech had exhausted him. The gathering dusk left a fragment of its sadness in the room, between them. Gazing at him he wondered at the old man, recounting at the end not his own life but his son's childhood. In any case, to pursue the difference between Tennyson and the Gita at this dim hour wasn't so simple. And, then, for the first time, he felt his own childhood crumbling away with the old man.

'Are you asleep?' he asked in an uncertain voice.

The old man's mouth had dropped open like a small pill-box. He shut it with a click.

'No—why?' he asked. A sheepish smile covered his face.

'Will you have something to eat?' he asked, although he knew quite well he never ate anything at night. But the old man started dozing off by the evening and he wanted to keep him awake so that he might sleep properly at night.

'You go and take a walk', he said, squinting at him in the dark. 'If I need anything, I'll call the nurse.'

He never walked very far. Not because he had premonitions, but because the very notion of a walk bored him utterly.

But sitting in the room was not without its dangers. Whether he was asleep or awake, the old man intuited his presence. He wasn't really looking for solitude, but the old man wanted to savour his 'vacation', it seemed, and he found it altogether intolerable to be with a companion.

He would leave the old man to his illusory holiday and sit out on a bench in the dimly lit corridor. And then he would suddenly remember his children. They were very young. He had almost forgotten them in the bafflement of the last few days. He thought it funny that they should be waiting for him to come back, as he was waiting for his father to go. Suddenly anxious, he would pull out his wife's letter and try to decipher it in the faint light of the hospital. Between the words he would fumble around for the woman's love that had been his desire a long time ago. He would reach out . . . and knock against the door behind which *he* was, smouldering in the darkness. That was when the fever rose, and he would sense someone standing behind the door. 'Go away—' the old man would mutter in English, '—Go away! Leave me alone! Go! Go! Go!', shrieking, as if wrenching himself free of a phantom. He would run out into the dark and then stop. In the corridor he would meet the nurse from Kerala who sailed in and out of the wards like some Florence Nightingale, carrying a torch instead of a lantern. It flashed into his eyes and blinded him for an instant.

'Where were you running to?' she would ask, surprised.

'To you!' he would burst out.

'To us?' She would look at him with interest. A

man of forty running through the dark corridor. 'Come along, we were about to make some tea. We were expecting you.'

At this time things eased up a bit, at eleven in the night. Their room was at the end of the main corridor, away from the other rooms. It had a broad couch on which two nurses could sleep side by side quite comfortably, and a picture on the wall—a tomb in Delhi nestling in a grove of trees—on seeing which he always remembered another time. Of sunshine and picnics, of girls laughing in the breeze. He would collapse face-down on the couch and sob. Go! Leave me alone! Go! Go! A voice would whisper, a voice etched on tape that he could hear any moment he liked. Quite distinct from the wailing of the jackals, so many jackals, for goodness sake! The jackals in March and the fragrance of the woods. And Mother stood there—Go, eat something, shove something down your gullet . . . How alone I am, Mother, and such a heap of life! An intoxicating smell enshrouded him, the smell from the nurse's coats which they had slipped off and flung over the couch. 'You've gone to sleep.' The Kerala nurse would tap him on the shoulder and he would jump up in confusion—'O no! I just dozed off for a moment. Have you finished your rounds?' The last night-round. She would part the curtain a little and in the torch-light peer at the patient, then come away. The entire hospital burned in an everlasting fever, it seemed, except this one room. Like the kitchen at home, glowing and yet cool. So cool, and here was the moment for a holiday, like those other days, like the clothes stripped off, strewn across the couch.

'You feel all right don't you?' she asked him every night.

'O yes, there's nothing the matter with me!' He was grateful. There is little enough to the ritual of tea, he told himself, but between a few cups it draws in an entire world.

'Do you come to Delhi quite frequently?' she asked.

'Not now, but I'm very familiar with the city.'

The Kerala nurse was one of those who put others at ease by their own easy manner, one of those towards whom one is drawn to confess everything, and at the very first encounter. About one's uprooted home, about the children growing up—but she would have to leave, and the confession was withheld. He restrained himself every night, noticing her fatigue. She slumped into the chair and lit her cigarette—she was the only one among the nurses who smoked—attempting to relax between the rounds.

'I've just come from your room.' She took the kettle off. The boiling water simmered.

He got up. His heart began to pound. 'Did you look inside?'

'Yes, I did. Why?' she asked.

'Did he say something to you?'

'What's he going to say! He's asleep.'

He's asleep. A damp curtain flapped inside him. No regret, no remorse, just a damp sort of terror. The sleep will escape soon enough and he will wake in the dark. There is not even strength enough in him to call out. Even so, he sat there, stopped shut the terror and sat there. I have the right at least to a cup of tea. He covered his face with his two hands. The few strands of grey on his head stuck out and shone in the light. What is happening to me! Foolish man, is this the time to think of my rights?

From the hill at the back of the hospital the wailing of the jackals rose, sounding like a knife scraping a sheet of glass, first one, then the second, echoing the first.

'Did your father work in a Government office?'

'Yes, all his life.' The word 'father' was pronounced by the nurse with much affection, as though she were asking not about his father but the padre in her village. For a long time he kept turning the word over in his mind.

'He speaks very good English—right out of the British days!' She chuckled. The signs of fatigue began to disappear.

'That's right. He lived throughout in Simla', he said with childish pride, as though there were some mysterious connection between good English and Simla.

'You must have been very young then.' The sister peered at him a little inquisitively, this man, crossing forty. More than the patients, it was the relatives she found intriguing. 'Very young?' she asked teasingly.

'Yes', he also smiled. 'I used to grasp hold of my father's walking stick as we went downhill—.' He had the desire to continue and say more about those days that stuck to the ground like stained leaves. But as soon as he reached out the old man caught hold of his hand . . . Leave me alone! For God's sake, leave me alone. And his hand hung in the air.

'Will you have some more tea?'

'No thank you, I'll go now.' But he didn't get up. The dry cool of the room held him back. The nurse was looking out of the window. The lights of the hospital twinkled softly in the darkened fields.

'Do you keep awake all night?'

'Not at all', the nurse said. 'If there's a new admission one has to keep awake, if there's none we sleep part of the night.'

'But if one of your patients—.' He started to stammer, warding off the word from his mouth like a fly. '—I mean, if there is something seriously wrong with a case—'

The nurse drew a long sigh. 'Such people become very quiet—there is no drama at the end.'

His body shuddered. 'At the end there's no—'

'Yes, they don't trouble us at that last moment.'

'All patients?'

'Almost all.'

He hung on the nurse's words for a while and felt himself grow lighter. Almost all, which means *he* too. He closed his eyes in the shadow of great relief.

'You will be going back, then?' The nurse found his sudden calm a little disconcerting.

'Going back where?' He put down the cup on the side-table with a trembling hand. He was tense again.

'I meant when the vacation is over', she said, reassuring him.

'Oh!'—he relaxed a little and laughed—'Yes, I have a family. I have children growing up.'

The nurse watched him in silence. Outside the hospital walls people belonged to such diverse worlds. This always seemed illusory to her.

'I wanted to ask you something', he said, girding himself.

'Yes, what is it?'

'I took ten days leave to come here', he said, swallowing hard. 'What do you think, should I extend it a few more days?'

'Why, are you uneasy here?' Suddenly her voice became thick and weary.

'Why should I be uneasy?' he asked defensively.

'No—well—'.

The reserve in the nurse's voice agitated him. 'No—look, I have no problems here, I'm quite all right, you know.' He felt his voice sticking to the howling of the jackals outside and he tried desperately to peel it off.

The nurse got up. A patient had rung the bell. But she stopped at the door. 'It is necessary for the sick man to stay here', she said in a low, clear voice, 'not so for you.'

He raised his head. No, there was no sarcasm in her voice, nor any sympathy. Only a cool essence that wiped the mist from the mirror. He also got up to leave.

He returned to the ward and lay down. Then sat up again. No trace of sleep. He switched on the torch. The round spot of light hovered on the wall. There was no movement in the bed across. As if it were empty. He bent the light to a page of his writing-pad, took a fresh sheet and started a letter to his wife . . . I am all right here. Don't worry about me. I stay in the hospital at night. I go home in the morning. Brother and I have arranged these shifts between us. Mother sometimes comes, in between. It is difficult to say how long I'll have to stay on here. Even the doctors don't know for certain. Tomorrow when they give him blood, I'll grab the opportunity and ask them—.

His hand stopped. I'll grab the opportunity, he read again, and then looked over at the bed, sunk in darkness. The nurse had probably given him a sleeping tablet, otherwise he wasn't one to lie there so quiet. He also lay down and switched off the torch. The darkness hanging over the old man's bed crept over to him. There was no sound in the corridor outside except the night nurse passing by with her torch. The spot of light touched the confused breath of the patient and dragged it along.

'Are you there?' The bed moaned.

'Yes. Do you need something?' His eyes were alert in the darkness.

'Will you wait here for a while? I'll be back in a moment.'

His voice, chastened by sleep and fever, shone like mercury. He sat up on his bed. Cold sweat trickled down his forehead.

'Where will you go? I'll come along with you', he said.

'Not you', the old man said. '*I* will go. But I'll return soon.'

'You won't go anywhere . . . this isn't home.' His voice shook with pain and vexation.

The man on the bed turned aside.

'Which home? Do you know how many homes we have changed?' the old man said.

The sleeping tablets have muddled him, he thought wearily.

'You didn't say which home.'

The wind swept through the corridor. Dead March leaves scudded about in circles.

'Is there someone outside?' the old man asked.

'No, there's only the wind outside', he said. 'Why don't you sleep?'

For a while there was a silence between them, then suddenly the old man sat up on his bed again. 'Will you agree to something?'

'Say it—'

'Take me home!' The old man's voice had dipped low.

He looked at him in the dark. Their breath was suspended in the space between.

'Are you afraid, then?' he asked softly. 'What is there at home that you miss here?'

'There's nothing there, that's why I want to go there'. The old man's voice had crawled near the edge of sleep and he sounded like someone dragged up after drowning . . . 'Here. . . here. . .' he started to mumble.

'Here, what?' he asked excitedly.

'Here it seems all of you are waiting for me.'

A black snake crept out from the thicket of breaths. He swallowed it down deep into himself.

Both of them were now sitting up. One on the bed, the other on the floor. In the darkness they both stared at each other.

'You don't say anything.' The old man mocked him.

'Do you know what time it is?'

'Will you let me go?'

'Won't you sleep?' His voice choked over a sob. He was afraid of himself now, in that darkness.

'You think I'm slipping. Give me your hand
. . . yes, touch me . . . come on, touch me I
say . . . you think I'll slip away!' In the dark his
laughter flashed out like a cat's eye. 'Touch me, yes,
don't be afraid. You aren't a child anymore
. . . touch, here, and here. . . . See, I'm *out*. I am all
outside. Look . . . where are your hands? Your
palms still perspire. Touch me, here on my hands,
my feet, my legs, my neck. . . *Grasp it*, grasp my
neck . . . No, no, I am not hysterical . . . I am not!
Touch me and see, I'm all out and exposed under
your hands. Will you let me go now? Tell
me . . . you won't stop me now!'

He started to touch his body. In the darkness. His
body was warm like trees after a shower. The limbs
shuddering and the veins stiff like tangled twigs,
trapping him, choking him, his own body splitting
up like straw in his father's ancient trunk. 'Let go,
then!' the old man shrieked in an inhuman voice, 'let
me be!'

And he suddenly remembered his children.

The old man quietened down, became numb all
over—the desolation of a father.

Then it all finished. The fever came down. It became absolutely still outside. Father and son flung
themselves down on their beds and stretched out,
panting.

Before he fell asleep a minute longing rose up within him—not even a longing, just a little tap inside—
that he should be able to say something, a word
perhaps, that *he* might use as a talisman. So that he
might unclose all that was shut for years, the warmth
of the kitchen, the rooms in the house, the mountain

breeze sweeping across the verandahs everywhere, where the dust had piled up, to open everything and look in—right to the very end.

The blood was falling drop by drop, finding its way into the old man's body, dissolving inside him. Whenever it stopped his brother shook the glass tube a little and the choked drops bubbled and travelled along the old man's arm once again.

Brother had taken leave from his office. He was acquainted with the doctors, he even teased the nurses a little. The shadow from the tree outside fell over the father's pillow. Swaying with the breeze, it moved across to the bottled blood and looked like a large butterfly trapped and fluttering in the red drops. He became dizzy. Coming out he sat down in the verandah, on the bench that his mother was sitting on. The same verandah where he had been caught running last night.

His mother looked at him and started to undo the bundle. He anticipated her. 'Not right away—' he hissed. 'I won't eat anything just now.'

Mother's hand froze where it was. She was afraid of his temper. And in any case over the last few days she had stepped back, withdrawn. As if they were all in a stage play where her children and their father had the major roles. And when they came back-stage, glowering and stamping, she would wipe their sweat, re-do their make-up, patch them up so that they might return to the stage.

'You fret too much. After all the illness *will* take its time', Mother said. Hearing her, cool and aloof, his gorge rose.

'How many days?' he asked. 'You seem to count the days!' He wanted to wring his mother's bland indifference like a wet towel so that it might shrink and crumple. Then he would be content—'*How many days*?' he asked again.

But it was a long time since that Mother had stopped listening to him. Now she tried to listen. 'Look', she said gently. 'Go home and rest a little. Chhote and I are here any way. If you are needed we'll call you.'

As though she were appeasing a stubborn child. He looked at her and sat on, his fists clenched. She had guessed what he wanted. This *was* what he wanted, but he did not get up immediately. He did not want to show how desperate he was to get away from the hospital, to get away even for a short while. Depositing the old man with his mother and brother, he wanted to be rid of him. How many years since he'd had a holiday, he wondered. At home he was driven by a desire to rid himself of his wife and children. Not all the time, but occasionally, like a toothache . . . But it is one thing to be free and quite another to swallow a pill and suppress the ache. There is no in-between freedom.

Inside the room the blood rose and fell. The old man floated in the stream of blood, unconscious. On the pillow the shadow of the branch swayed again and sent down a shower of scarlet drops. A fly hovered above the patient's face persistently, like the little bagatelle ball which goes round and round and then settles each time in the same hole.

Without saying a word, he came out. He came out in something of a rush, as if to piss—as though he were rushing out to rush back.

Coming out of the hospital compound he slowed down, quaking a little at the thought of going back home on an empty afternoon to an empty house. Over the last several years his friends and acquaintances had gradually dispersed. And if he ever chanced to come upon one of them his heart sank. After the initial formalities they would only gape at each other. The thought that they were, *all* of them, living on as before, baffled him. And then life suddenly loomed up like a mountain, and all of them seemed to be ants climbing up the slopes, one after another, sniffing each other in a long trail, up and up, with their families behind them. . . Climbing up to reach the spot where his father lay at that moment gasping for breath.

He was getting breathless but he walked on, hoping the further he went from the hospital the quicker freedom would approach him. Behind the hospital there was an open stretch of land known as Bhooli Bhatiari. A Youth Hostel sporting flags from different countries and hippie boys and girls stretched out in the sun. The fields were covered with dull brown shrubs. Smoke rose from the dust-laden gypsy camps nearby, where women sat about, ripping their children's hair in search of lice and bugs. A mixed odour of flesh and garbage hung about the place, enough to turn one's stomach, so different from the cool, civilized smell of the hospital. The blue roof of March over the world, and above the open roof nest-like clouds . . . *he* would not see all this, now. The old man knew nothing now, his system absorbing drop by drop the petrified blood of an unknown body.

He sat down underneath it, soaked through; underneath the scarlet shadow of his father's blood. Above him there were the kites, the doctors, his mother . . . waiting. There was home, yes, Babu's home.

'Listen take me home!' Down the hill. Long ago. He would catch hold of Babu's stick and climb down, for Babu had been drinking. Stumbling, he would climb down, climb up, and then down again. First the slope of the Mall, then the sharp decline near Kali Bari. He would steady Babu's stick every now and then. 'Munne baba, I've drunk a lot today!' And Babu would laugh. In the club he would drink with his friends, and the boy would stand apart—he would stand by the window, looking out towards the Simla lights, hazed by the snow. Anyone seeing them in the midnight snow would have been amazed. A startled little boy dragging his father by the walking-stick down the hill. Their breath would turn into clouds of smoke in the snow. Reaching the Mall Babu would get excited, snatch away the stick from the boy's hand and swing it in the air as if the stick and not he himself were tipsy. 'Munne baba!' he would say, 'do you know why the English made these steps going right down to the lower bazaar? But what can *you* know. You weren't even born then!'

He would stop, peer at him, and then, for a moment, turn quite severe. 'Long ago, when they built Simla', he would continue, 'only the English could walk on the Mall. If ever an Indian strayed up, the police immediately shoved him down the steps, to the lower bazaar. It's true!' He would double over laughing, put his arm round the boy's neck—'don't walk so fast! See, I can't breathe, I am breathless!' He would get on to speaking English—'look, don't run!

My breath. It's running out . . . it comes and goes . . .'.

A brittle breath. After so many years, it's still around, crawling through his oblivion . . . scalding the white hospital bed . . . brushing over the bed-pen, soaked in blood and sweat and urine.

He returned, running, as though he had finished an appointed task. As soon as he entered the hospital compound he was relieved, rid of the shades hovering about him. For the first time in the last ten years he was idle, and empty—empty and open, and returning to himself. How strange—this day of March, drawn from the remote past, and he had not lost anything at all. The things he had long forgotten were all there, secure in their niches. At the right moment they came out, flapping their wings, and perched themselves on his shoulder. All that he had sealed for good was ripped open in their beaks. And he ran around after the torn rags, to catch them, grab them. Listen, my breath . . . it comes and goes . . . Are you listening?

At the entrance of the ward he met his brother who had been waiting for him but didn't ask where he had wandered the whole day.

'You look a little tired', the brother said. 'You should have slept at home last night.' He himself looked worn and sad. His heart went out to his brother.

'Are they continuing to give the blood?' he asked.

A vague dread passed over the brother's face. 'They'll give half the blood tomorrow—if his condition remains okay.'

'If the condition remains all right?'

He looked anxiously at his brother. His breathing broke. 'He can't sustain all of it', the brother muttered softly. They gazed at the fading light outside. It faded but did not darken. He felt then that their father's illness was a kind of support, that they might lean on it together. No drama involved. There were questions, of course, but they stayed with Babu. Until he gave the cue, there was no purpose in saying anything further. *He* is purposeful man, he'll finish off. But he won't undo his bundle of purposes.

'Here is the bundle', the brother said. 'Mother has left some things for you. Eat a little. Before going to the office tomorrow I'll look in to find out. You must try to sleep. There's no point . . . you'll fall ill.'

Before leaving he looked in. Under the yellow light-bulb Babu's nose glistened like an ancient cliff amid new sites, and the breath climbed up and then climbed down.

'Don't worry', he said, tugging at his brother's shoulder, 'I'm here, I'll be with him all night.' The brother looked at him with vacant eyes, crossed a stretch of desert and then stopped, reaching a little patch of green where once they had been children together. 'Look, if anything happens, you call me. I'll come immediately. Don't hesitate. Nothing will happen, but even if there is a hint—I mean a single person is alone after all whereas two people—and listen, keep changing the sheets, I mean, he keeps lying there drenched and the nurses don't bother.'

He felt like telling his brother—*you* stay. If you are so concerned, stay one night, one doesn't know which night will be the last. He is a little scared of *you* at least. He considers me an outsider, argues over every trifle. You'll say he loves me all the same. You've always nursed this in your heart, that he loves me more. But if it won't upset you I'll tell you something. I'm through with his love—really. He feels embarrassed, as though it were shameful to love, and I feel queer in turn, and nervous.

But he said nothing and the brother did not stay. They talked perfunctorily, and beyond that the desert stretched out again. The conversation proceeded like bare feet on scalding sand. Hurriedly stepping ahead the brother passed him by, and he was left standing behind under a ragged shadow. On one foot, then on the other, as though no relationship was ever cool enough for him to put down both feet at the same time.

He sat with the bundle in a corner of the room and began wolfing down the food. The day's hunger sprang up suddenly. He glanced at the door as he ate, and then at the old man's bed, like an animal in the zoo snatching at each morsel, keeping an anxious watch beyond the bars, afraid someone might interfere. But the interference came from his own heart. It was peaceful outside. The peculiar, oppressive silence of the hospital after the guests have all left and the patients withdraw and meekly crouch back into their beds.

His hand stopped in mid-air. The morsels of food worked in a see-saw mastication of jaws.

The night nurse poked her head into the room— 'No, no, keep eating please, I just came to look in. Is he asleep?'

'Yes.' His courage jumped three feet and now took an inch-step forward. 'He doesn't usually sleep at this time.'

'There's nothing to worry.' A familiar expression

of weariness settled on her face. 'He's had blood,
that's why he's tired.'

As she was going a savage dread came over him—
the kind of fear that has no form but an acrid taste.
'There's nothing to worry!' he chuckled vengefully.
'No sir, whyever will I worry?' Like an idiot he repeated the nurse's sentence.

'If you need anything, I'm in the duty room,
okay?' she said. Unusually tender, as though he had
chided her with his laugh. Then she turned round and
left.

His laughter hung there and stiffened. He would
avenge himself to the last on these people! Rushing in
whenever they pleased! He couldn't eat any more.
Tying up the bundle, he began picking up crumbs
from the floor. On an impulse he thought, let me
sweep the whole room clean. But he stopped for fear
he would wake up Babu with the noise. *Let sleeping
dogs lie.* These crude English phrases, how they popped up in his head at the oddest moments. A childhood habit he hadn't outgrown. He unfolded his bedding and lay down. Sleeping dogs stretch out in
streets and you have to step around them, cautiously.
Bastards. How they lie there in the scorching heat
with their jaws agape and their red eyes closed shut,
tongues lolling, dribbling saliva, panting. For a long
time he listened to panting breath from the bed beside
him. About to drop off, it would jolt him, and the little sleep he had gathered with such difficulty escaped
at once from the leaks like a gutter-stream.

And then everything would begin to flow. The
nurses' laughter from the staff-room, from the corri-

dor the sound of eddying leaves that came tapping at
the door and then hushed. . . Those crazy March
leaves. The trees shedding their leaves and with it the
city too, shedding off. Delhi where he used to come a
long time ago to do his examinations. Stiff tortilla
leaves on Delhi streets began to lift and scatter, whirl-
ing in the breeze, and they reminded him of examina-
tion days. Clean, bright, wrapped in yellow foil. And
under his arm Babu's notes, which he had specially
prepared for him.

Exam days and notes were also fragments scudding
away. Outside the hospital jackals wailed and joining
their cries he woke up with a start. The sound came
not from outside, but from inside the room. The old
man was weeping, oblivious of all else, as though
alone. Trembling, he put his hand on the bed to seek
him there, where he lay. He was not panting now.
His uprooted breath had settled down and crouched
in the corner, exhausted. It seemed the ascent was
over and he was now coming down. Why this sobbing, then? As if it were a shame to come down. He
bent down to support him, reaching out to grip the
handle of the walking-stick. In the dark his hand
knocked against the drip. A quick faint tingling leapt
between them like lightning.

'What is this you're doing?' Babu yelled out at
once.

'I thought—'

'Don't think, go to sleep. If you need my sleeping
pills, take them—leave me in peace!'

He sat down at the spot where he had stood. And
should he take the sleeping pills? Once again that
grimy age-old fury shot up its hood. It started crawl-

ing about, ripping away the layers, grating the flesh, releasing the blood. He felt he was again the little boy with his shoes in his hands, climbing the steps, quietly stealing up so as not disturb Babu's sleep. But Babu was already standing at the top of the steps, waiting for him, not sleeping, just watching him climb up, shoes in hand, like a thief—come, come, you can't fool me! He was laughing. In those days he would laugh without reason.

He was weeping.

He had a mad wish to find his way out of both options—of his laughter then, and now his weeping. And then he stiffened. He felt himself winning. Because he is alive, he is winning—this realization came to him with a horrible start. The mere fact of being alive can be a victory. Without avenging oneself, without struggling. A contemptible victory, but true nevertheless, solid stuff, something that wouldn't let go of you even if you wished to let go of it.

He grabbed at the switch and put on the light. The bed gleamed. At the edge of the sheet there were a few dark spots. The blood they had given him in the day had spattered on the bed here and there like betel juice, which turns dark as it dries.

'Did you have a bad dream?'

'Bad dream? You're crazy!' the old man hissed.

'You . . . you were crying.'

A spot of light hovered between them. They were facing each other. At their back, somewhere far off, there was a clamour of dry leaves, playing up the silence of the corridors.

'When you were little you used to perspire in your sleep.'

'I still do', he said.

'I know, I watch you every night.'

'You watch me when I'm asleep?' There was an aversion in his voice, not from hatred so much as from regret.

'We used to change your sheets', his father said.

'Don't reminisce about me—look into yourself', he said in a trembling voice.

'I'm looking into myself. Do you ever do as much?' He laughed in a vulgar sort of way. O Lord! At this age. He had an impulse to catch hold of his father's hands and jolt him. But he kept sitting. A moment before he was winning but now it seemed there was nothing. He sat there, clinging to the wall of nothing. Like a lizard that you poke with a stick and it scrambles into one corner, then to another, but won't come off the wall.

Maddened, he returned to his bed. But he did not lie down. As though half the game were still unplayed. He was not going to run away during the intermission, he would go along with the old man to the very end. Play his bluff to the last wager, when he had no option but to declare his cards or throw them down.

'If you're going to sleep switch off the light', he said and turned over.

He came near the bed to switch off the light.

'Listen. . . '

'You want something?' His hands stiffened.

'I beg your forgiveness', his father said.

He felt his father was laughing again. Not with his words but with his face, not with his face but with his inert body—which is what he had become, was slowly becoming.

He picked up the stone and there was no 'forgiveness' underneath. There were some ancient worms and things that began to writhe in panic when exposed to the sunlight. Quickly he covered them up again.

'What sort of forgiveness', he asked in a hoarse voice. '—What is this you're saying?'

'I was thinking—' Babu's tone had humbled somehow. 'I was thinking how you are always strung up in anger.'

'Listen, *you* don't worry about me.' His voice dropped. '—I am quite happy.'

'You don't seem so.'

'I'm as happy as I can ever be', he said, as though praying before the old man. The old man did not hear him. He had veered off somewhere. In the middle of a conversation the rope snapped and Babu floated away to the other shore. . . He tugged at the rope so that he would return, dredged up from the mists of half consciousness, smeared with mud and slime.

He smoothed out his bed and placed the torch beside the pillow. Then in the darkness he groped around in Babu's bed and felt relieved that the sheets were not still wet. There was a damp patch near the back, the sort one often finds in the beds of old people and little children—not sweat, nor urine, a milky moist odour wiggling over the body.

For a while both of them lay smothered by this odour. The night nurse looked in. There was peace in the room. They were both breathing evenly, the breathing neatly strung together. She felt no apprehension. She turned and walked back with a soft step, leaving the door ajar so that she might rush in if necessary.

That necessity arose. At midnight. When the wind had started up again across the grass patch which the patients' guests had left littered. Soiled newspapers, peanut shells, dead cigarettes—in the dark everything swam in the breeze.

'Where is your mother', he whispered, half unconscious. 'I mean, where should she be at this time? Listen, she can't abandon me like this. Shall we go, then? This is the month of March—do you remember? You were born in this month. Your mother and I and you. . . ' He tried to get up.

'Where? Where are you going?'

'I'm returning. No, no, leave the Gita alone, its quite useless! No. Don't misunderstand me. I've always believed—But at this point there isn't any use for it. We must go to the very end. The Gita is meant to hold you mid-way, not to take you to the end. . . There, to the end, the dog goes. Listen, don't grab me like this. I'm not running away—you. . .'

'What on earth are you doing—and at such a time?' He held him down with both his hands. The old man was struggling. 'Wait a moment, I'll call the nurse. She'll set you right. O Lord! Can't you get to sleep. Okay, don't sleep, speak on, I'll listen to everything—so many people fall ill—but not like you—.' He began stuttering in his rage. '—They don't go crazy like you!' The sweat poured from his forehead. His voice turned into a whimper again. 'Look, after all, where *are* you going? Good Lord! You are being theatrical, you know? And in the middle of the night. . . *Shame!*'

The old man looked up at him, blinking. For a long time he looked at him vacantly. Then, slowly, he spoke in English. 'I am ashamed of you! Did you hear that, or shall I repeat it—? Its not just today. I have always been ashamed of you—of *all* of you!' A thread of saliva drooled and reached his neck where the flesh hung in two white pouches. Over the white flesh, making its way through the blue veins. He went numb and watched him, fascinated. The thin snake slithering over the face. Then a hideous fear gripped him. 'Why did you stop? Speak! You can't shut off like this. Look—you are ashamed of us— And then? Speak! No, you can't just go like that, d'you hear? This isn't your home where you do what you please. From here you go nowhere!' He began giggling and buried his head between the old man's shoulders. Then he tried to resuscitate each of his limbs. '. . . speak! You can't go like this . . . speak! speak! speak!'

The nurse stood at the door. The spot from her torch found two interlocked bodies.

For a second she couldn't distinguish the visitor from the patient, the man who was left from the man who had gone.

*Translated by Geeta Kapur*

# The Burning Bush

I had come to that city for the first time. I thought I'd stay there a few days and then go on, but some unexpected business forced me to stay longer. I remained at the hotel all day and every time I felt bored I wandered over towards that spot. Even in a strange city travellers seek out a favourite corner. . .

So it was that, several times, I felt like going there. While looking around in the evening for a cheap restaurant I often gazed in that direction. Sometimes, while the tram was crossing the bridge, I looked out through the window and could feel a powerful attraction surge up within me. I wanted to get down there and then, but each time I'd hesitate and hold back.

But that day must have been different somehow. I slept in my hotel all day. Then I wrote some letters and went out on the pretext of posting them.

On my way back I intentionally took a different street. I suppose that in some vague way I felt free—that often happens. When I go out after sleeping all day I feel an urge to take off in a new direction, especially in a strange city where no one recognizes me and where I can turn from one street and follow another without constraint.

It was on one such day in autumn that I went there.

It was an island on the edge of the city where the hilly section began. Like the blades of a pair of scissors, the two branches of the river had cut it out between them. There was tall grass standing in the water under the bridge and some red benches stood in a row along the bank. The benches were usually empty at that time of year. Not entirely empty—leaves fell on them endlessly. When a gust of wind brushed these off, others would fall on the benches as the wind turned back. They could never stay empty very long. The water continued to flow, and along with the voice of water another was heard: 'Some day I will go to that spot.'

And so I went to that spot one autumn day.

While walking along the bank I kept my distance from some boys playing under the bridge. They probably didn't even see me. They had made a pile of leaves, were lighting it with matches and running away. Circles of smoke rose in the dim evening light. A fragrant aroma floated all over the island.

I walked away from the bridge, over to the other side of the island where the bare branches of the trees touched the water. Some sections of the wet grass went down to the edge of the river. As I descended the slope my eyes suddenly caught sight of him. I stopped abruptly.

He was an old man, seated on a small camp-stool, completely motionless and silent. A pipe which had died out long ago was clenched in his mouth. There was a fishing rod in his hand; its line was sunk far out in the muddy water of the river. But his attention was not focused on the fishing rod. Instead he was looking across the island at the bridges of the city. The pipe in his mouth quivered.

It was a peaceful corner of the island. I had grown tired after wandering aimlessly around. Putting my leather down on the damp grass, I sat down.

There was a bare-branched tree next to me, soaked by the rain but warm. I began to take in its warmth gradually. It had been raining in the city the past week. The ground was wet under the grass and so soft that it seemed the trees were sinking down into the earth.

It was the day after the rains had stopped. There were still some clouds in the sky, some above the islands, some lingering over the hills of the city. But now they were empty and light and appeared to be flying in the breeze.

I remained sitting there for some time. All that time the old man didn't catch a single fish. The rod shook once and he swiftly grabbed it. I thought that a quivering lump of flesh would emerge soon. Indeed I suppose I had become quite excited, for I slid down to the water. But nothing happened. He lifted the rod from the water, then looked at me and laughed. The hook was empty. The fish had very neatly stolen the bait and escaped.

Then, silently, we both sat down, back in our respective places. The old man filled his hook with bait and, swinging back the rod, flung the line high in the air. A wide circle spread out over the water—it glimmered like mercury in sunlight and then disappeared.

He lit his pipe again and pulled the collar of his old overcoat up to his ears. A fragment of sunlight floating on the water whirled round like a top, hit the bank and broke apart. But the old man didn't even glance at it. I tried to tell exactly where his eyes were fixed but couldn't. I couldn't even tell for certain whether his eyes were open or closed.

But bit by bit my suspicions ripened. What those suspicions revolved around I can't say exactly, but they must have pointed to some subconscious doubts. He had looked at me and laughed only once, but I wondered if even then he had really seen me. Yet, if he hadn't seen me, why had he turned towards me and felt the need to laugh?

I was beginning to feel strangely uneasy. My presence was completely unacknowledged by him, even though I sat very close to him. This seemed extremely odd to me. Till that moment I hadn't fully realized how much one longs for friendship in a strange city.

His eyes were no doubt fixed on some particular thing somewhere, which, if it was within my frame of vision, I hadn't yet spotted.

I tried to spot it. Directly before his eyes was the oldest bridge of the city, beyond this the slender walls and roof of the National Theatre, and between these the bridge towers gleaming in the twilight. But these were things one saw every day walking in the city and strolling through the lanes. There was nothing special about them, nothing out of the ordinary, at least not for the old man who must have lived in that city for years. The suspicions within me were roused—perhaps there was something else, something entirely different. . .

But can this man see at all? The sudden thought jarred me. He is very old. . .

A slight gust of wind blew by, the light was beginning slowly to fade away. An inert heaviness was falling over the whole island. Some leaves had dropped down into the water and were floating past. Only scattered spots of sunlight remained, on rocks and on branches. A little later, evening would sweep them away. Only the two of us would be left there.

But no—he was going. I looked up quickly. He was actually leaving. He had drawn in his fishing line, folded his camp-stool and stuck it under his arm; then he put on his ancient yellow derby and removed the pipe from his mouth, sticking it into his pocket. He hung his empty fishing kit from his rod.

For some reason, at that moment, a queer shiver ran through my body. I felt I was in some intricate and mysterious way dependent upon him—as if by his leaving I would lose something which had been living in me for a long time, as if his staying here was itself tied to my staying here. . . But at just that moment something must have happened, perhaps the rustling of some withered leaves or perhaps a stone tumbling into the water. He was alarmed, as though his feet had suddenly got tied to the ground, as though someone had caught hold of him. Turning around at once he looked at the flowing water of the river, and then moving rapidly walked away from me.

As he left he did not once look at me. For a while I continued to hear the crushing of leaves under his feet. . . Then, as before, everything became silent.

A few minutes must have gone by in this way. I stood up and, going over to precisely the spot where the old fisherman had been sitting, sat down. The impressions of his shoes were still visible in the mud— they were not very long but rather wide and a little crooked in the front. They seemed quite ordinary to me and I did not look at them much longer.

Quite some time passed I suppose. I tried to collect my thoughts as I felt rather confused. For some minutes past I had in fact been staring blankly and aimlessly in the very direction that the eyes of the old man had been turned. Some birds were flying above the bushes along the bank. The last rays of the sun were sparkling on the windows of an old church across the embankment, their reflections glittering in the river like red, tear-filled eyes.

No one could know, I thought to myself, no one could know that only a short while ago the old man had been sitting here, right at this very spot. I found some comfort in the thought that I was free of him. It was entirely possible that the whole thing had been my mistake, a delusion such as often arises while wandering about a strange city. As soon as I returned to the hotel room—when I found myself alone at a new beginning—everything would return to its normal, proper shape.

A tram was crossing the bridge in front of me, the reflections from its lights gliding on the water like sparkling beads. Some of the passengers were looking out through the window at the island in a casual, natural way, just the way I would look while going by. But now, seeing people's faces at the windows, I began to have doubts about myself—as though I had done something wrong by coming here. I felt that I too should have continued straight across the bridge.

If I made an effort, I could still leave, only. . .

I heard the sound of light footsteps behind me. The boys were walking slowly towards me. Like other boys in the city, they wore round blue caps on their heads. The smaller boy had a large coloured handkerchief in his hand in which he had collected some dead leaves. The larger boy, taller than the other but apparently not much older, was walking along, casually waving a small branch in the air. Both had reached the end of the island where the bushes along the bank touched the water.

The smaller boy carefully descended the bank and tossed the leaves from his handkerchief into the water. Then, emptying more leaves from both his coat pockets—soggy and muddy leaves—he floated them on the water. As he was doing this I felt the larger boy look at me, still waving his branch in the air. All this while he chewed on a blade of grass stuck between his teeth. The smaller boy climbed back up after having floated all his leaves. Both were now standing together, looking at me.

There is a sort of gaze, a direct and steady gaze, which catches us and draws us in, like a reel. I often feel this way—the gaze transfixing me just as a needle transfixes a worm which, dazed at first, soon becomes frantic and finally quietens down, hypnotized, unconscious. It was like that; yes, exactly like that.

The larger boy then came nearer, approaching me in an easy manner. His coming up to me in this way seemed as completely natural as though I'd been expecting him.

'How are you today?' he inquired. I was about to say something when I noticed that the boy standing in the background was smiling with a detached sort of expression.

'Empty-handed?'

I looked down at my hands at once. They were indeed empty.

'I don't mean that', the larger boy declared in that same natural and controlled tone. 'Didn't you catch anything again?'

'But. . . You're mistaken. I'm not the man you're looking for. He left a long while ago.'

'Where?'

I looked around. The dusky, pale redness of the sinking sun had spread all over the island. In the distance, by the bridge, smoke was still rising from the pile of burning leaves. But he was nowhere to be seen. There were only the windswept leaves, tumbled from the benches and now rolling on the ground.

'He isn't here any more', I replied; but this time my voice, curiously, was not as firm as before.

'But you come here every day', the smaller boy asserted. 'Look there, we can still see one of your footprints.'

I looked. A footprint was still clearly visible—wide and a little crooked in front. In the trampled and torn-up grass the sharp and full impression of a shoe. Like the amputated limb of a body, the footprint was embedded in the wet ground.

'But it's not mine', I protested in a weak and unsteady voice. He remained standing there silently. I felt he was waiting for me to take a step forward to prove this. That could have been done quite easily, but something prevented me. With all the strength I had I kept my feet hidden in the grass.

Nothing happened after that. They seemed to lose interest in me. The smaller boy moved away and was collecting fallen leaves in his handkerchief, as he had been doing before. I think that the larger boy must have stayed there a few minutes longer, completely indifferent and detached.

Then, all of a sudden, I felt stunned: he was standing on the very spot on which the old man had stood transfixed for a few moments when about to leave. Exactly the same spot, and his eyes were fastened on the same unknown point at which the old man had stared for such a long time.

This was probably only a coincidence, nothing more than that; for a moment later he kicked a clod of earth into the river. The water shook. Somewhere far beneath the surface many different layers were stirred up. On the wet ground by the bush a line of crawling insects stopped for a minute and then continued their march forward. He spat the blade of grass into the water. Taking his cap off his head he tossed it in the air a couple of times and put it back on again. Then, waving his branch in that same casual fashion, he started off after the other boy.

And that was it. He went, leaving me by myself. Once again there I was, alone; but after they'd left that former feeling of solitude didn't come back. As long as we have that solitude to commune with, even when we're with others, then, in any real sense, we're not alone. But now I had only myself, alone, and I was frightened by the thought that those two had robbed me of something which had been a part of me.

I could not sit there for a long time after that. I went back again to my old place next to the tree trunk where my bag still lay. How anxiously and easily we discover security!

By now the hills of the city were lost in darkness. But rising above them were the smoky spires of a Gothic church, suspended in the sky like a half-forgotten dress. As I looked at them they seemed to resemble a gigantic bird abruptly halted in flight, his wings bent up between the hills and the open sky, petrified in mid flight.

At some distance from the island the lights of the old bridge of the city were coming on hesitantly, one by one. Their reflections glimmered in the flowing water like shimmering candlelight.

Had I ever before met those two boys who had left just a minute ago? But I was a stranger in the city. If I left suddenly this evening, except for the hotel manager and the police no one would notice. No, I was under some delusion. Surely they hadn't recognized me. Such errors often happen. Perhaps they were playing a joke on me. Boys often play jokes on strangers.

I was rather glad they'd left; yet I consciously suppressed this happy feeling as though I were ashamed of it. A few dying flames were rising from the burning leaves. The boys had deserted the fire long ago. And now there was silence everywhere, constant and unceasing as the sound of flowing water. Meanwhile the line between the island and the river had been erased, or perhaps not—but it was difficult to make out the water in the darkness. As I gazed intently I could see a pale whitish liquid carrying along the evening breeze, lingering sometimes and then jogging the reflections of the bridge lights on the water and slipping away.

The cold abruptly increased. I was about to leave

when I sensed that I wasn't completely alone. By the bush on my right I heard a low rustling sound. At first I could make out only two hazy shadows; then I saw each one distinct and separate. The front of the girl's skirt had probably got caught in the bush and she had bent down to pull it loose. The rustling of the bush had probably drawn my attention to them. There was another person a little behind her whom at first glance I could not distinguish very clearly, perhaps because he stood motionless and silent, and because his long overcoat merged with the dark so that without straining my eyes it was impossible to recognize his separate form.

I thought I should get up quietly and leave. I knew that at nightfall pairs of lovers frequently came to the spot. Of course there would have been no danger in my sitting there if they had seen me for they would then have been aware of my presence. But in the present situation, with me looking at them and they assuming they were alone, it seemed disgusting to stay. But before I could make up my mind they had disappeared into the bush.

By then a heavy and unbroken silence thickened over the island and even a low voice in the distance carried distinctly. The bush was quite close to me, hardly three yards away. And the deep fitful breathing of the couple soon reached me from there. A burning heat poured from the bush, piercing the air and penetrating it; then, twisting like a spellbound snake, it coiled around me. The bush shook again and again as though it could not bear the weight of their warm, heavy breathing. Under them, crushed leaves continued to crackle. A repressed scream, a sobbing moan, then not even that—a light, cool breeze, and everything was as peaceful as before.

Thinking it over now I still don't know why I didn't leave. Whatever went on behind the bush didn't really matter to me; I felt no aversion, nor even curiosity. But even so my feet would not lift themselves. I remained seated, as if paralysed.

A little later they emerged. Or rather, I guess I felt that both of them came out from the bush, though I could see only the girl clearly. She rearranged her hair and carefully picked off the leaves and pieces of grass stuck to her skirt. Then she walked away from the bush towards the river. I could hardly suppress my astonishment when I realized that she had sat down on the very spot where first the old man and later I had sat.

I looked at her. She lit a cigarette. Her hair was very short, like a boy's. She was wearing a black unbuttoned raincoat, and I could see her skirt slipped up to her knees under it. She blew out the smoke with a tight, repressed sigh, her eyes still half-closed.

'Did you see?' she muttered softly.

I kept quiet.

'I thought you'd gone', she continued.

'Did you say something to me?'

She started laughing. 'Is there anyone else here?'

She still wasn't looking at me. She was looking across the river, staring at one fixed spot. I suddenly remembered that the old fisherman had been gazing in the same direction—beyond the bridges and the church spires where the lights of the city stopped and the darkness began.

'Did you come earlier?' she asked.

'I . . . I was right here.' She looked straight at me when she asked me that and this time I wasn't as startled as before.

'And there?' She turned around and pointed at the bush.

I didn't understand and looked curiously at her.

'I didn't go there alone.'

Again she started to laugh. This time her laugh was different, unpleasant, full of mistrust, as if she'd caught me. It was as though when, knocking on the wrong door by mistake, someone grabs your hand and pulls you inside before you can leave.

'But your companion?' At once I was afraid. My eyes turned swiftly to the bush. The entwined branches had been partly separated by the wind, and the entangled leaves were torn open. Recognizing someone is not difficult. I would recognize him, and then she'd realize I wasn't the one she thought I was.

'He is there; I saw him with you', I said firmly.

'Where did you see him?' A very nervous, timid hope appeared in her voice, as if she were greatly dependent upon my answer—as if the thread of her fate was tied to my words. . .

'Where did you see him?'

'Look in that bush there, I . . . he is there now.'

'Who?'

The bush trembled, as though something deep inside it were burning.

She moved closer towards me. . . Was I really myself? I heard a soft rustling, like a page within me being turned over.

And the final page . . . after that there was nothing.

I felt this was the second time that evening someone had demanded that I prove my 'truth.' The bush was only three yards from me, probably less. It would have taken a couple of seconds to reach it. I could take the first step, then a second, and then it would be directly in front of me. Each step would take me closer to the bush, where he was, where he still was.

It wasn't a difficult thing to do. There was nothing to be afraid of. It was so simple and natural that my heart started to beat faster. I would take just one step and not stop to think; I would take a second step and then—then it was meaningless to think of fractions of time. I had reached the age when such small bits of time were meaningless. Look here, I said to myself, look here, she is waiting for you. She was holding her breath, looking at me sceptically. I almost felt it was the boy chewing the blade of grass still staring at me.

I stand up—I move towards the bush. Her eyes are glued to me. To this day no one has looked at me with such impatient and alarmed eyes. There is a sort of gaze which catches us and draws us in. This is not that sort. While she looks, she is pushing me away, separating me from her. And I hesitate, pull myself back, stop. The moment of accountability comes upon us suddenly, when we least expect it; we think it has come for another, not for us; if not for that other, then for a third person; if not for the third, then for a fourth, a fifth, a sixth person—for anyone, but not for us. It seizes us, though, with trembling hands. But we are strong and free ourselves from it and think it is all a bad dream. Once we open our eyes we see just what we want to see. . .

I begin to run. I begin to run and do not look back.
The bush is behind me and her cruel ghostly laughter
which follows me like drops of blood dripping behind my running feet. . .

I could not go back to the hotel that night. I spent
the night making the rounds of the bars. I sang with
the drunks, my arms around their shoulders. Then,
exhausted, I'd fall asleep in a bar, be dragged out and
left in the street. Then after a while another drunk
would take me to another bar. And so in this way I
continued to wander through all the dark lanes of the
city, sleeping, walking, singing, being dragged out
into the streets.

The morning of the next day I left the city for good
and moved on.

*Translated by Susan Neild*

# A Splinter of the Sun

Can I sit here on the bench? No, please don't get up. I'll sit at one end. You're perhaps surprised that I don't sit on another bench. The park is so big, there are so many benches lying vacant, and yet I thrust myself on you—isn't it? I must tell you, if you don't mind, that the bench on which you're sitting is in fact mine. Yes, it's here I sit every day. Please don't take it amiss. I don't have my name written on it. How can one—on a municipality bench? People come here for a short hour or two and then go away. No one remembers who sat where in the park. After they leave the bench is empty, as before. When someone else walks up a little later he can't tell whether a schoolgirl or an old lonely woman or a drunken gypsy sat there before him. Oh no! Only those places have names where men settle down for good. That's why houses are often given names—even graves. . .

Ah, you're looking at that victoria over there? Well, don't be surprised. People do still use victorias on their wedding day. I see this one often. That's why I picked out this seat. Straight ahead of you is the church—you don't have to turn your head. It's an old church. A wedding here is a prestigious affair. People have to reserve the place some eight months in advance. I feel though that the period between the engagement and the marriage shouldn't be that long. It could strain a relationship beyond endurance—even, perhaps, with neither of the two turning up on the appointed day. Such days are rather depressing you know. The street lies empty: no crowds, no victoria—even the beggars go away disappointed. On such a day I saw a girl on the bench opposite. She sat alone, her gaze fastened on the deserted church.

That's what is strange about a park. Out in the open people sit cooped up within themselves. You can't even speak a word of comfort to anyone. You look at them, they look at you. Maybe this in itself is some sort of solace. It may be the reason why people tired of the loneliness of their rooms come out into the street and go to a public park or a pub. Even if there isn't anyone to comfort you out there at least your grief moves and turns on its side. Not that your burden's less, but you do shift it from one shoulder to the other. And that isn't a trivial respite, is it? I know it's not—and so I leave my room early in the morning. Please, don't misunderstand me. I'm all right, I'm not unhappy. I come only for the sun. You must have noticed this is the only bench in the park which isn't under a tree. No leaf falls here to disturb you. It has another advantage: the church is right in front and you can see it . . . but perhaps I've said that before.

You're lucky. You've seen a victoria on your very first day in the park. Soon you'll see a small crowd gather in front of the church. Hardly any among them knows either the bridegroom or the bride. None the less they wait for hours to catch a glimpse of the newly-weds. I don't know how you feel, but I think there are some things you never stop being curious about. For instance, as you wheeled in the pram I immediately wanted to see your child, as though he were any different. Actually all children of this age are the same—they keep lying on their backs in much the same manner, sucking at their comforters. Still, I can hardly keep myself from peering into a pram as it passes by me. One is never too tired to linger a glance at children in prams, at newly-weds in their victorias, at the dead in a cortege. You must have seen crowds of onlookers at all such places. I sometimes wonder how the things which affect us deeply elude our grasp. We can neither understand them nor speak to anyone about them. I ask you: can you recall the moment of your birth, or tell anything about your death? Can you repeat to yourself the experience of your married life in its varied entirety? Why, you're laughing. . . I wonder if one can recall the moment when one decided not to live alone any longer. I mean, can anyone—can you put your finger on the point in time when you let the loneliness in you shift over to make room for another person? Like you made room for me on this bench a little earlier? And now I'm sitting here talking to you as if I'd known you for years.

Look, some cops have joined the group outside the church. If it goes on swelling like this it'll hold up the traffic. We've warm sunshine today but I've seen shivering people standing about expectantly on cold days. I've been seeing all this for years now. Sometimes I suspect the men in the crowd over there are those who came to my wedding in this church fifteen years ago. The victoria appears the same, the same cops stroll about on their quiet beat. Nothing seems to have changed ever since. Yes, I was married here in this church. It was so long ago, it might have taken place in another age. This street was narrow then. You could't drive up to the church in a carriage. We had to leave it behind in the other street and walk the gauntlet of curious eyes. My father was with me. My heart pounded like mad. I was afraid I might slip and fall on all fours. I can't tell where those men have gone now. D'you think if one of those men who watched me walk to the church in my bridal white saw me now sitting on this bench he'd recognize me? Tell me, can anyone? I don't know about the men, but that brace of horses would surely recognize me. Yes, horses puzzle me. Have you ever looked into their sad, mournful eyes? It seems to me there's no misfortune greater than not becoming used to your lot. . .

What did you say? No, I don't have a child. I'm lucky not to have one, for then perhaps I'd never have separated. You must have seen how an estranged couple pull on religiously together for the sake of their children. I've had no such encumbrance. I'm happy in this respect—if happiness means the freedom to choose one's loneliness. It's a different story, though, to get used to it. When the sun withdraws from the park I withdraw myself to my room. But on the way back I always go into the pub where he'd wait for me in those days. Do you know the Black Horse? That's the pub. When he first asked me to wait for him near the Black Horse I spent the whole evening with an equestrian St Wenceslas at the other end of the city. Have you, on your first date, spent a whole evening waiting outside a pub while your girl is far away mooning for you under a public statue? Later his likings became my habits. We'd spend our evenings together at the pub where before he'd met me he'd sit alone; or we'd go for a walk in the part of the city where I grew up. Isn't it funny that when you fall in love you want to share the present with your man, but you also want to sop up his past, when he was alone? We become so possessive and jealous we can't even bear the thought that they could once have lived a full life without us—loved, eaten, slept, made merry, and so on. Later, after you've lived together a few years it becomes almost impossible to say which of your habits is yours and which you've acquired from him.

Listen, I think one should be given a chance to dissect oneself before one dies. Peel off the past like the layers of an onion. You'd be surprised to find how everyone—your parents, friends, husband—comes claiming his share, until you're left with nothing more than the dried up stalk which is either cremated or buried after you're dead. It's often said that one dies alone. I don't agree. On dies with all those who were inside one, hated or loved. One goes with a whole world within. That's why you're sad when someone dies. It's being rather selfish though, for you mourn the part of you that will disappear forever with his death.

Look, the child has woken. Rock the pram a little. It will quieten him. . . How he lies with the comforter in his mouth, like a fat little cigar! See how he's staring up at the clouds! When I was a little girl I'd twirl and wave my stick at the clouds as if they moved at my bidding. . . What do you think? Can people remember what they see or hear as children? I think they do, in spite of themselves. Certain snatches of conversation, certain glimpses, certain sounds, which, though later lost in the maze of routine-bound years, return as if with a vengeance, just when a person, unawares, walks down a street or waits for a bus or lies in bed over a moment suspended between sleep and wakefulness. You hardly know what has struck. I know it. It has happened with me, too. That night. . .

We were sleeping together when I heard an unusual sound—something like what used to pull me out of sleep in the middle of the night in my room as a child. I'd come awake with a start and be afraid my parents weren't there in the next room, that I wouldn't ever see them again, and I'd begin to scream. I got out of bed and went across the room to the door, opened it and looked out. There was no one out there. I made my way back to the bed. I rested my eyes on him. He was sleeping with his face towards the wall, as on the other nights. Obviously he hadn't heard the sound. Then it struck me it hadn't sounded out *there*, but within me. It hung around, fluttering its wings like a bat, somewhere between inside and outside. I sat down on the bed. I touched him. I touched him in all the places that had given me comfort earlier. But that night I was surprised for my hand returned empty from its quest. The reverberations that surged from his body some years back and tingled up my hands into my heart weren't there any more. I touched him, as other hands touch ruins in search of names they have earlier carved there. My name was nowhere around. There were some other imprints, some graffiti I hadn't seen there before. Nor did they have anything to do with me. I sat there almost the whole night near his pillow, my hand lifeless on his body. It was frightening to realize I couldn't speak of the emptiness between us to anyone, not even to my lawyer.

My lawyer thought I was going nuts. What sound? D'you think your husband is unfaithful? Is he seeing another woman? Is he cruel?. . . Oh yes, he showered the questions at me while I gaped at him like an imbecile. Then it occurred to me it wasn't necessary to go to courts to obtain a separation. They say one's grief diminishes when shared with others, that one's load becomes lighter. I never felt light though. People never share the grief, they pass judgement. The trouble is you've broken with the only one who could read your pain. So I left that part of the city and came here among the unknown. No one here points me out to another saying: 'This woman left her husband after eight years.' Back over there I could hear such remarks, and then I'd want to catch hold of the people and tell them all that passed between the two of us from beginning to end. I'd want to tell them how on our first date he'd waited for me outside the pub while I spent the evening in the company of a public statue. I'd want to tell them how he'd stood me against a tree and kissed me that first time, and how timidly I'd reached out my fingertips to touch him on his head. I'd feel I must tell everything from scratch to make them understand the nature of the leap of fear in my heart that night, the nightmare which pummelled me to my father's room years ago . . . That room is empty now. I've read somewhere that growing up consists in waking alone in darkness: you scream but no footsteps hurry to your door, no one comes from the next room—it always remains empty. See, how I've grown up!

Look here! Tell me how it is that news of an earthquake or bombardment is splashed across newspapers and everyone knows next morning about the heap of rubble in place of the school building and about the dust blowing over erstwhile ruins. Yet when something like this happens to a person no one suspects it. The morning after, I roamed alone all over the city, and no one as much as threw me a glance. . . The first time I came to this park I sat where you're sitting now. And I was surprised when my eyes caught the church over there. I was married there. But of course in those days the street wasn't wide enough for a victoria. We'd had to walk down. . .

Can you hear the organ? Look, they've thrown open the doors now. The music floats up on the air. As soon as I hear it I know they've kissed each other and exchanged rings. They'll come out in a minute or two. The crowd's becoming impatient. If you want to see the couple you may go, by all means. I'll stay here and look after your child. What did you say? Yes, I'll be here till sundown. It becomes cold and I must leave then. I stay here till the sun does. All day long, I'm on the lookout for a splinter of the sun. I go from bench to bench with it. There's no place in the park I haven't been to. But I like this bench the most. For one thing, leaves don't drop on you here, and for another . . . What, are you leaving already? Listen . . .

*Translated by Kuldip Singh*

# The World Elsewhere

Long ago I knew a girl who played all day in the park. There were many trees in the park but I could name only a few. I would spend the whole day in the library and in the evening when I came out I would find her sitting among those trees. We did not speak to one another for many days. I frequently place-changed those days for cheaper accommodation and had settled in that corner of London only for a short time.

London seemed wretched and I felt low most of the time.

The girl in the park looked no better. She was always in a threadbare sweater. An auburn cap covered her head but her hair tripped out rebelliously from both sides. Her ears and the tip of her nose seemed a permanent red as those were the last days of October— days just short of winter—and sometimes those early days were more cruel then the acutal winter.

I went to the library only to thaw out my frozen bones. At night before retiring I'd wrap myself in all my sweaters and socks, and for additional comfort I'd pile my coats and overcoat on top of the quilt—but still the cold would not go. Not that there was no heater in the room, but it took a shilling to light it. The first night I spent in that room I fed the bloody thing with my shillings throughout the night. I had no money even for breakfast the morning after. Then I left the heater alone. I shivered through the nights but I had the consolation that the heater too lay there, cold and starving. And so the cold war continued between us night after night.

With the first hint of the morning I'd hurry over to the library. I've lost count of the many others who like me were regulars there. They stood in a queue long before the door of the library opened. They were mostly old people who received a meagre pension. They'd open a book or two and settle down at the table. After a while I'd hear them snoring softly. No one disturbed them. Occasionally an employee of the library would go round, close the open books and gently pat those whose snores disturbed the sleep or study of others.

On one such slumbering noon I saw that girl from one of the windows of the library. She had put her satchel on a bench and hid herself behind the trees. It was a cloudy afternoon and she was all alone. The other benches were empty. And that day for the first time I became intensely curious, wanting to know the games children play when they are all alone.

She would come to the park at noon, put her satchel on the bench and run away behind the trees. Now and then I'd raise my head from the book and watch her. The hospital clock would chime at five and the girl, wherever she was, would rush and return to her bench. She would hold the satchel in her lap and wait with deceptive calm till she discovered a woman walk towards her from the other direction. I could never see the face of the woman. She was always in the white uniform of a nurse. But before she could wend her way to the bench the girl would run and meet her halfway. They would turn towards the gate and my eyes would follow them until they had both disappeared from my sight. All this I watched, like a Hitchcock hero, out of the window, where this pantomime was repeated everyday. This scenario would have continued perhaps all through the winter had the weather not taken a turn.

One night I suddenly felt choked under the weight of my quilt and coats. I was perspiring as if recovered after a long bout of fever. I opened the window and peered out. There was no mist or fog; the London sky lay open like a blue velvet-box filled with stars. I felt as though it were a summer-night and I were lying on the terrace of my own home.

The next day was gloriously warm. I could not sit in the library for long. I got out at noon and walked down to the restaurant where I ate every day. It was a cheap Jewish restaurant where one could get kosher meat, two slices of bread and a small glass of beer for just a shilling and a half. The Jewish proprietress who came from Lithuania before the war sat on a high stool. The cash-box lay on the counter; a Siamese cat crouched under it staring at the customers. She blinked at me with her little green eyes as I ate. Perhaps she had begun to recognize me. Even a cat, I reflected, is a great help in times of destitution and loneliness. Some day, my thoughts completed their circuit, I too would set up an Indian restaurant and keep three cats as pets.

Coming out of the restaurant I lost the desire to go back to the library. I had received letters and newspapers from home after a long time. I wanted to read them in the park's sunlight. I was a little surprised to see flowers in the park. They were tiny flowers, their heads bravely erect in the grass. Perhaps it was these flowers that Jesus had called 'lilies of the field'—flowers that do not despair of the morrow.

They reminded you of a long gone summer.

I walked on the flowers scattered in the grass.

It was very pleasant. Nightmares of the future were forgotten. I felt light. I slipped my shoes off and began to walk barefoot in the park. I was almost near the bench when I heard a shriek behind me. Somebody was rushing towards me. I turned—it was the same girl. She emerged from the cluster of trees and blocked my way.

'You are caught!' She was all excitement. 'You cannot escape now.'

I didn't understand. I stood still where I was.

'You've been caught . . . ', she repeated, 'you are standing on my land.'

I looked around. There was the grass, the flowers, empty benches on one side, three evergreen trees and an oak tree with a heavy trunk in the centre. There was no trace of her land anywhere.

'Sorry', I said and turned to leave.

'No, no . . . you can't go', the little girl stood barring my way. Her eyes were shining. 'They won't let you go.'

'Who won't let me go?' I asked.

She pointed to the trees, which now took on the appearance of tall and sturdy guards. Unwittingly I had fallen into their invisible trap.

We stood facing one another for some moments. Her gaze was fixed on me—excited and alert. When she saw that I had no intention of fleeing she relaxed.

'Do you want to be released?' she said.

'How?' I looked at her.

'You'll have to give them food. They've been hungry for many days'. She pointed to the trees. Their woolly heads shook against the breeze.

'I don't have food with me', I said.

'You could bring some if you want to', she advised. 'They eat only flowers and leaves.'

It was not difficult. Those were the days of October when besides flowers there were plenty of leaves scattered all over the park. Just as I stooped she sprang forward to intercept my hand.

'No, no . . . not from here. This is my land. You'll have to go over there', she gestured towards the park fencing where wizened leaves lay in a heap. I started in that direction when she called.

'Please, wait . . . I'll come with you, but if you try to escape . . . you will die at once.' She stopped, looked at me, 'Do you want to die?'

Hastily I shook my head. It was such a warm and bright day that I had no wish to do any such thing.

We went up to the fence. I took out my handkerchief to collect the flowers and the leaves. It was the least I could do to buy my freedom.

She was quiet as we walked back. I glanced at her from the corner of my eye. She seemed to be a sickly child. Grim, as children are who play alone. Her lips twitched when she was silent—the lower lip protruded slightly, above which her pug nose appeared

pathetically helpless. Her hair too short, and too
black, parted like the rings of washed cotton, and
there was this uncontrollable urge to touch them.

'Now you may feed them.' She had stopped near
the trees.

'Will they release me?' I wanted some guarantee,
some assurance.

This time she smiled and for the first time I noticed
her teeth—pure white and shining, the kind black
girls have.

I took the leaves from my handkerchief, divided
them into four parts and distributed them equally at
the foot of the trees.

I was free—and somewhat empty too.

I took out the letters and newspapers from my
pocket and sat down on the bench where her satchel
lay, a black leather satchel crammed with books and a
half nibbled apple straining out of its upper pocket.

She had vanished. Cautiously I looked around and
caught the briefest glimpse of her frock behind the
shrubs. She was crouching like a rabbit, ready to
pounce upon another straggler like me. But no one
passed that way for long. The leaves deposited under
the trees swirled like an eddy as the wind blew, and
she ran after them, forgetting her ambush.

She came to the bench after some time, regarded
me for a moment and took the apple out of her bag. I
heard her munch the apple as I read my papers.

Suddenly she noticed my letters lying on the
bench. Her jaws stopped moving.

'These are yours?'

'Yes.' I looked at her.

'And this?'

She pointed to a stamp on the envelope, inscribed with a picture of an elephant, his trunk raised high in salute. The space between his tusks suggested laughter.

'Have you ever been to the zoo?' I asked.

'Once with papa. He gave me a penny and the elephant picked it up from my palm with his trunk.'

'Weren't you scared?'

'No, why?' she looked at me, nibbling her apple.

'Doesn't papa come here with you?'

'He had come once. And was caught thrice.'

She chuckled—oblivious of my presence—as one would in solitude where a single memory peels off the past in layers.

We were both startled when the hospital clock chimed the hour. The girl picked up her satchel from the bench and walked alongside the trees which stood in silence. She went to each tree, touched it and muttered something which only the trees could hear. Finally she came to me and shook my hand, as though I were also a tree in that family of trees.

She glanced back. I looked to see who it was and saw the woman. The familiar white uniform of a nurse gleamed in the sun. As always, the girl ran to accost her midway. I took in the details—this was the woman I had watched from the library window. Short of stature, a bag slung over her shoulder and curly black hair like the girl's. They were some distance from me but their voices floated back as a muffled suggestion of two sounds and not as words articulated separately. They sat down on the grass. The girl had forgotten me.

I wore my shoes and put the letters and papers in

my pocket. There is yet time I thought. I could still spend an hour or two in my solitary corner at the library, away from the magic of the park.

I ambled over to the centre of the park. The stems of the trees were aglow and the entire park melted in gold. In the centre a river of leaves rippled in the breeze.

'Who, who's there?' Someone was calling me. I walked on. I did not stop. Sometimes people call out to seduce themselves to step inside while there is only a void within. But this call was different, unlike calls of other days. It did not cease. It forced me to stop. There was no doubt this time. Someone was really shouting, 'Stop, stop . . . '. I turned round: the girl was waving her hands in the air.

Indeed I was caught again! Like a fool I had trespassed on her land, surrounded by the four trees, for the second time. The mother and daughter were both laughing this time.

It was a false summer. Everyone knew it wouldn't last long. The library was deserted. My neighbours, the cold pensioners, sat outside in the sun. The sky was so blue that even the London smog could not dirty it. The park underneath lay like a green island.

Greta (that was her name) would be there all day. Even when she was out of sight her satchel on the bench hinted of her presence somewhere, perhaps crouching in some corner. I walked warily, wary of the trees, the shrubs, the flowers on the grass. Every day she would leave some invisible dangerous trap, and when for all my caution I put my foot in it she would emerge from nowhere screaming madly. I was caught, released, caught again . . .

It wasn't a game. It was a world in itself. I had nothing to do with that world—though I was permitted entry, sometimes, like an extra in a play. I had to be ready all the time for she could summon me any moment. One afternoon we were both sitting on the bench. Abruptly she stood up.

'Hello, Mrs Thomas . . . ', she said with a smile, 'I haven't seen you for a long time . . . Meet him, this is my Indian friend.'

I watched her dumbfounded. There was nobody there.

'What's the matter with you? Shake her hand', she scolded.

I stood up and shook hands with the empty air. Greta sidled closer to me to make room for Mrs Thomas.

'Were you going shopping?' she said, glancing at the empty spot. 'I guessed from your bag. No, excuse me, I can't come with you. I've got a lot of work. Look at them (she signalled towards the trees), they've been hungry since morning, I haven't yet cooked for them. Will you take tea? Coffee? Oh, you've had some at home. I beg your pardon—why don't I come to your house? Where's the time these days! Hospital in the mornings, afternoons with the kids, you know how it is. I'll come on Sunday. What, are you going already?'

She stood up and shook her hand again. Perhaps Mrs Thomas was in a hurry, she did not notice me as she took our leave. In turn, I remained seated.

For some time we sat in silence. Then suddenly she started.

'Do you hear something?' she shook my elbow.

'No, nothing . . .', I said.

'The telephone—how long it has been ringing! Please see who it is.'

I rose and went behind the bench, picked up a twig and said aloud, 'Hello!'

'Who is calling?' she asked anxiously.

'Mrs Thomas' I said.

'Oh, Mrs Thomas again!' She yawned wearily, dragged herself to me with slow steps, snatched the twig from my hand and said, 'Hello, Mrs Thomas— you're back from the market? What did you buy? Meat-balls and fish-fingers and potato-chips?' Her eyes widened with interest. Perhaps she was picking the delicacies of her own choice.

Then she fell silent, as if Mrs Thomas had made an unexpected offer. 'All right, Mrs Thomas, I'm coming right away. No, I won't take long. I'm on my way to the bus station. See you soon, Mrs Thomas.'

She beamed at me.

'Mrs Thomas has invited me to dinner—what will you do?'

'I'll sleep.'

'First give them something to eat lest they cry.' She pointed to the trees which stood motionless in the still air.

She started getting ready. She combed her dishevelled hair, powdered her face in a splendid mime and held up her palm to see her mirrored reflection. Caught between the sunlight and the shade of the trees, she looked beautiful.

She waved a goodbye as she went. I watched her

until she disappeared among the trees beyond the hedges of the park.

This became a daily routine. She'd go to visit Mrs Thomas and I'd lie on the bench. I didn't feel lonesome. I was always surrounded by the invisible voices of the park. I'd watch the clouds over London, gliding aimlessly and casting dark shadows in the park each time a stray white patch drifted over the sun.

One such day as I lay on the bench I heard a strange rustle beside me. I felt as though I were watching Mrs Thomas in a dream; she was close—very close—to me and calling me.

I woke up with a start.

In front of me stood Greta's mother, holding her hand and staring at me awkwardly.

'Excuse me', she said, embarrassed, 'I hope I didn't disturb your sleep.'

I stood up, brushing my clothes.

'You're early today', I said. The sight of her white uniform, black belt, and hair held together by a scarf, dazzled me. It seemed she had arrived straight from the hospital.

'Yes, I'm early', she smiled. 'There isn't much work on Saturday and I come here in the afternoon.'

She spoke with a broad West-Indian drawl in which the last syllable of each word took off like a balloon.

'I came to ask if you'd like to come home with us for tea today. We live nearby.'

There was no hesitation or pretence in her tone, as though she had known me for ages.

I agreed. I had not been to anybody's home for a long time. I had been shuttling between my bedsitter, the library and the park. I'd almost forgotten that there was a world beyond, where Greta lived and ate and slept.

She walked ahead of us. Now and then she looked back to make sure we were not lagging too far behind. She probably felt a little odd that I should be on my way to her house. I felt odd too, not because I was going to her house but because I was walking along with her mother. She looked quite young, possibly on account of her height. She looked so petite walking beside me that I had the illusion of walking with another Greta.

She was quiet on the way. Only when we reached their house did she abruptly stop and speak.

'You also live somewhere here?'

'In Bride Street', I said, 'just opposite the tube station.'

'Perhaps you've moved in recently', she said, smiling, 'there are very few Indians in this area.'

She started climbing down. Her home was in the basement and we had to descend the staircase to get there. Greta was already there, holding the door open for us. It was dark inside the room even during daytime. Three or four chairs swam into view when the light was switched on. There was a table in the middle—longer than was necessary and bare, as if used for playing ping-pong. Close to the wall lay a sofa, a quilt neatly folded at its headrest. It looked like an all-purpose room, meant for eating, sleeping and on occasion entertaining guests.

'Please sit down. I'll just get the tea.'

She raised the curtain and went in. Greta and I remained alone in the room. We had started recognizing each other in the autumnal light of the park. But inside the room we became strangers.

She suddenly turned into a very young child whose magic and terror both withered away.

'Do you sleep here?' I looked at the sofa.

'No, not here', she shook her head, 'my room is inside—would you like to see it?'

There was a smallish room opposite the kitchen which must have functioned as a store in the past. It was behind a blue chick on which hung a bluish placard—'Keep Britain tidy, but leave my room alone!' She raised the chick and stole inside.

'Please come quietly, he's asleep.'

'Who?'

'Hush!' she put her hand on her mouth.

I thought there was someone inside. But the room was empty. The walls of the room were green, pasted with pictures of animals. In the corner was her cot, which looked like a crib. A teddy bear was lying on the pillow, wrapped in rags, like a cameo.

'He's asleep', she whispered.

'And you?' I asked, 'don't you sleep here?'

'I do. When Papa was here he used to sleep on another bed. Ma has now had that bed put away.'

'Where does he live?' This time my voice was also soft, not for any fear of the bear but for a fear I had reared within for many days.

'In his home—where else?'

She looked at me with some amazement. She felt I wasn't entirely satisfied. She went up to her table where her school books lay. She opened a drawer and produced a bunch of letters. Tied with a red ribbon, it looked like a Christmas gift. She brought the bunch to me and gestured to the stamp on the top envelope.

'He lives here', she said simply. She was mimicking me. I recalled, long ago in the park, I had shown her a letter from my country.

Her mother was calling us from the sitting room. She went out as soon as she heard the voice.

I did not move for some time. The bear was sleeping on the cot. The eyes of the animals on the wall stared back at me. There was a small basin by her bed where she kept her toothbrush, soap and comb.

Just like my own bed-sitter, I remembered. Yet altogether different. I could leave my room and go anywhere; but her's looked almost eternal in its belongings. On the table lay the bunch of letters tied with a red ribbon which she had left all alone in a hurry.

'Did you see her room?' Greta's mother asked with a smile.

She had changed her clothes. A red chintz skirt and a loose brown cardigan. The room was redolent with the smell of cheap scent.

'This is not tea, but a feast!' I said, looking at the items on the table. Toast, jam, butter, cheese. I didn't know when I'd last seen so many things together.

'I got these from the hospital canteen—they are cheap there.'

She looked worried. She laughed, but traces of the worry remained. I wondered where the child was. She was yelling for her and the tea was getting cold.

She sat holding her head in her hands. Suddenly she remembered I was there too. 'Carry on, please.

She must be in the garden.'

'You have a garden of your own?' I asked.

'A tiny one, at the back of the kitchen. It was a de-relict piece of waste when we came here. My husband cleared it. And now it's producing some veg-ables.'

'Your husband doesn't live here?'

'He didn't get a job here—he would wander all day in the park. Greta has picked up the same habit.'

There was a slight weariness in her voice. Devoid of any annoyance of course, but a weariness never-theless, which settles like dust on everything.

'Well, I too lounge about in the park', I said airly, wanting to make her smile a bit. And I did. She laughed.

'You are different', she said, 'you are alone. But with a family it's impossible to live in London with-out a job.'

She began to clear the table. I gathered the utensils in a heap and carried them to the kitchen. A window against the sink looked out into their garden. A weeping willow stood in the centre, its branches swinging like the spokes of an inverted umbrella.

I saw her as I turned. She stood at the door, a towel in her hand.

'What are you looking at?'

'Your garden . . . it is not that small.'

'It's not . . . but the tree has grabbed the entire space. I wanted to fell it, but she was adamant and spent the night crying.'

She fell silent, as though the recollection of that night was a matter of profound grief in itself.

'What did she say?'

'What could she say . . . she simply wouldn't let me do it. Her father might have told her long ago that they'd build a summer-house under the tree—now, you tell me how can we make a summer-house for dolls in the garden when we don't have enough room for ourselves?'

'A summer-house?'

'Yes a summer-house—where Greta would live with her bear.'

She laughed, a sad, melancholic laughter that rose from a void and ended in another void, leaving the intermediate space empty.

It was time for me to leave, but Greta did not appear. We went up the stairs. The murky sunlight of London was slithering up the neighbouring chimneys.

As I held out my hand to take leave, she said with some hesitation, 'Are you free tomorrow?'

'Well, I'm free almost every day.'

'It is Sunday tomorrow', she said. 'Greta has a holiday, but I have to go to the hospital. May I leave her with you?'

'When should I come?'

'No, please don't bother. I'll leave her in front of the library on my way to the hospital and take her back when I return later in the evening.'

I nodded and stepped out on to the street. After I'd walked some distance I took out the money from my pocket and began to count it. I was happy I'd saved on dinner. I pressed the small change in my fist and walked homewards.

I was standing at the door of the library.

They were late, perhaps on account of the cold. In the absence of the sun a faintly discernible patina of light covered the buildings of London—a pale, yellow light that made them look even more derelict and sad. I caught a glimpse of her white uniform. They were both coming through the park. She in front and Greta running behind her. She waved as she saw me, gave Greta a swift kiss and hastened towards the hospital.

But there was no sign of hurry in the child. She took her time coming to me. Her nose was scarlet in the cold. She wore a full-sleeved brown sweater and on her head the same old cap that I'd seen so often in the park.

She stood there, looking exhausted.

'Coming?' I took her hand.

She nodded quietly. I was slightly dismayed. I had thought that she would at least ask 'Where?' But she asked me nothing and we set out to cross the road.

She looked questioningly at me as we left the park behind us: for her it was like going out of her charmed circle. But I told her nothing and she did not pursue her mute inquiry. I realized then that when children are not with their parents they make a parcel of all their queries and throw it in some dark hole.

She looked somewhat reassured as we got into the tube. She left my hand and began to look out of the window.

'Is it night already?' she asked.

'Why night?'

'Look, it's so dark outside.'

She mused, then said softly, 'It's night below, and day above.'

Both of us laughed. This had never struck me before.

Gradually we saw the light. A patch of sky first and then the day, bathed in endless sheets of white, hurtled toward us as we came out of the tunnel.

She stopped while climbing the stairs of the tube station. I looked at her in surprise.

'What's the matter?'

'I must go to the bathroom.'

She stood, her hands between her legs, looking as if she were on the verge of a crisis.

I shuddered. The toilet was downstairs and it was doubtful whether she could have walked that far without making a mess. I lifted her and rushed back down the staircase. The toilet for gents was at the other end of the corridor and I hustled her in. When I closed the door behind me I felt a tremendous surge of relief.

She looked perturbed as she came out. 'What's it now?' I asked.

'The chain is too high' she said.

'Wait here, I'll pull it.'

She hung onto my coat. She wanted to pull it herself. I went in with her, picked her up and raised her high until the chain was within her reach. We watched the water gushing down the toilet with wonder, as if witnessing this miracle for the first time.

We climbed the steps a second time. She held my hand tightly when we reached the top. Trafalgar Square lay before us, crowded, bright and noisy. I wanted to give her a surprise. But she was frightened. She was so frightened that I almost led her back to the tube station where the earth contained a secure darkness.

But soon her fright melted away, and after a while she released my hand. She was lost in the marvellous light of the square. She ducked under the lions who stared intently at the passing crowd, their claws splayed out on the black stones. Some children fed corn to the pigeons. The shadows of their wings looked like clouds carried by air currents to different directions. Passing overhead they'd leave behind a hot, sharp flutter in the ears.

She was listening. She'd forgotten me.

I sneaked past her to the centre of the square. There was a cabin made of redwood where corn was sold for four pence a cup. I bought a cup and searched for her in the crowd.

There were many children surrounded by the pigeons, but she stood where she was. She hadn't budged an inch from her place. I went behind her and held out the cup of corn.

She looked at me with surprise. Children are never grateful, they merely accept. A third eye opens that levels down all silences. She nearly snatched the cup from my hand and asked, 'Will they come?'

'They'll certainly come . . . you'll first have to throw the grains one by one to tempt them to come, and then . . .'

She didn't hear me. She ran in the direction where a couple of pigeons hovered absently. In the beginning, she stretched out her palm rather timidly. The pigeons hesitated, as though her timidity had touched them too. But they couldn't restrain themselves long. Abandoning their gimmicks they came closer—feigning indifference, a look here and a look there—and began to pick the grain briskly from her palm. She was now sitting with her frock spread on the ground. The cup in one hand and corn in the other. She was out of my sight now, the grey fluttering ceiling of wings had canopied her from view.

I sat on the bench and watched the fountains, whose water came flying up to my knees in haphazard drops. The clouds hung so low that Nelson's head looked like a black speck.

The day wore on.

After a while I found her standing before me.

'I'd like to have one more cup', she said.

'No more, now', I said with some hesitation. 'It's quite late. We'll have tea—and you'll have an ice-cream.'

She shook her head.

'I'll have one more cup.'

There was no obstinacy in that tone. As though the intimacy which had developed a few moments earlier was urging, not me, but her.

I took the empty cup from her and started for the shop. I looked back, she was watching me. I went behind the shop. It was crowded and her eyes could not reach me. Slipping into a corner I took the change out from my pocket. I put aside some money for tea and ice-cream and for the tube; I was left with only two pence. I added some money from the tea fund and queued up in front of the shop.

This time when I gave her the cup she didn't even glance at me. She ran off immediately to the spot where there was the largest cluster of pigeons. Now her spirits were high. And the pigeons had begun to recognize her. Flying around, they'd perch now on her hand, now on her shoulder, and now on her head.

She laughed unceasingly, her pale face almost distorted with a feverish strain. And her hands, those hands which had always seemed so helpless to me, opened and closed with a strange restlessness, as if they'd grab the fluttering, fleshy throbs of the pigeons any moment. She did not know when the cup emptied. She continued to sit for some time, her palms stretched out in the air. Suddenly she realized the pigeons had left her and were now flocking to other children. She got up and without looking in any direction walked towards me.

'We shall go now'. I got up from the bench.

'I'll have one more cup.'

'No, not any more—you have had two.' I was annoyed. 'You know how much money we are left with?'

'Just one, and then we'll go home.'

People were staring at us. I was arguing over a bowl of corn. I picked her up and sat her on the bench. 'Greta, you're so obstinate. Now you won't get anything.'

She looked at me coldly.

'You are a bad man. I'll never play with you.' I felt she was comparing me to some invisible person. I sat down, feeling empty. There are times when there seems to be no hope for oneself. Only an extreme bewilderment at one's being—one is bewildered because one is. Then I heard a sound which I hear even now in solitude, and turned my face.

She was crying. The empty cup was in her hand. And her cap was askew on her forehead. It was a lament in silence. I couldn't bear it. I took the cup from her hand walked off to join the queue. This time I did not even think of counting the change. I heard only her sobs, though she was quite a distance from me. Moreover, the flutter of pigeons and the screams of the children drowned out every other sound. Yet above and beyond all this was a dreadful quiescence within me, holding in its centre her choked breathing—and this I could hear from an endless distance.

But this time there was a difference. For a long while no pigeon came near her. They'd come close but perhaps because of her mounting nervousness, or perhaps, again, because of the gathering dusk, they'd fly away to the other children, ignoring her open palm. In desperation she left the cup on the ground and came away to sit by me.

A flock of pigeons flew to the cup as soon as she had left. After a while we noticed that the cup lay careened, empty of grain.

'Will you come now?' I said.

Immediately she got up, as if she had been waiting only to be asked. Her eyes gleamed, a wet gleam which comes after tears.

Those days there used to be a Lyons Restaurant in front of the square. It was both dirty and cheap. We crossed the street and went in.

In the meantime I had counted the change in my pocket. I ordered two toasts for her and a cup of tea for myself. It was best to forget about the ice-cream.

This was her first visit to a restaurant. She looked around, deeply curious. I felt that the anguish of the past few moments was melting away. We were again close to each other. But not with the same intensity— the shadow of the pigeons still fluttered between us.

'Am I such a bad man?' I asked.

She lifted her eyes, watched me for a moment, and then said rather anxiously, 'I hadn't meant you.'

'Not me?' I looked at her, baffled. 'Then who did you say that to?'

'Mr Thomas—he's a bad man. One day when I'd gone to their house he was yelling and poor Mrs Thomas was crying.'

'Oh!' I said.

'And you thought I'd said that to you?'

She began to laugh, as though I had blundered. I don't know why, but my heart sank when I saw her laugh.

'Shall we come here again?' she said.

'In summer', I said. 'We shall go to the Thames which isn't far from here.'

'Will there be pigeons there?' she asked.

So like a girl's repeated reference to her lover that it hurt me. But I hated to disappoint her again. The summer was far, we had still to go through autumn and the days of snow. By then my lie would melt away, I thought.

Although the afternoon was not yet over there were traces of dusk in its maw when we emerged from the restaurant. She looked absently at the square, where the pigeons were still flying. I had money barely enough to scramble home in the tube. Mercifully, she made no demands. I have a feeling that beyond a certain limit children are able to sense the misery, if not the poverty, of grown-ups.

I had thought I would ask her about the summer-house when we boarded the tube, and about the willow which stood majestically alone in her garden. I wanted to bring her back to her own world, where we had first met one another. But this did not happen. Her eyes grew heavy almost as soon as she sat down. It was quite a distance from Trafalgar Square to Islington. After a few moments she leaned her head against my shoulder and fell asleep.

I briefly studied her face. I was amazed to see that she looked the same as I had seen her first, among the trees in the park, absorbed and intact. The restlessness that had surfaced with the pigeons was no more. Her tears had long dried up. In sleep she looked as secure as she did in the bushes. And then an odd thought came to my mind. She had ensnared me a number of times in the park. But looking at her intense face I felt that while people like me are caught rarely, here was a girl who had always been trapped. She was not aware of it, which was fortunate because the adult is always under the illusion of being set free, of being released, while the child has no such hope. Then for the first time I had the courage to caress her. I touched her cheeks, warm after tears, but she slept.

The rain, which started on that night, continued for a week. The days of a false summer were over. The city lay shrouded in layers of a pale mist. One could see nothing while walking on the road—trees, lamp posts, or people. I remember those days because that was the time I found a job. It was my first job in London. The load of work was heavy, though not tough. I had to stand at the counter of a pub for seven hours. I had to clean glasses of beer and spirits. I had to ring the bell at eleven and drive out the drunkards. I could not go anywhere for some days. I'd return home and take to bed, as though sleep would resolve an old feud. Whenever I opened my eyes I saw the rain, which, like the incessant ticking of a watch, continued without respite. Sometimes I had a feeling that I was dead and listening from the other end of my grave to the patter of falling rain.

But one day I saw the sky, not all of it, but just a blue, sunken slice, and suddenly memories of the days in the park, of the cat in the Jewish restaurant and of Mrs Thomas on her way to the market, flooded back. It was a holiday. I put on my best clothes and got out of the room.

The library was open. All the old faces were there. The park was empty. The rain of previous days glistened on the trees. They looked somewhat shrunken, as if the rumour of impending winter had touched them.

I waited till the afternoon. Greta was nowhere to be seen, either on the bench or behind the trees. The pale, autumnal glow in the park was fading out. The hospital clock struck five and my eyes involuntarily turned towards the gate.

The last rays of the evening lit up the iron handle on the gate, and the red-brick hospital building loomed large behind it. I knew that she had to walk through the park to get home, and yet my eyes wandered uncertainly from the gate to the road. I also thought that perhaps it was her day off and they might both be home.

The street lights came on. I felt strangely nervous, as though the end of the waiting had arrived and I was avoiding it. I stood up from the bench—it seemed easier to wait standing up. But just then I heard a movement near the gate. I spotted her uniform even before I saw her face. She was walking briskly along the footpath in the middle of the park. She had not noticed me. Even if she had come in my direction, she would perhaps not have recognized me in the twilight.

I ran behind her.

'Mrs Parker.' It was the first time I had addressed her by her name.

She stopped, momentarily taken aback when she saw me. She had recognized me but seemed unable to grasp the meaning of this recognition. I felt a bit awkward and said in a normal voice, 'You are returning rather late today. It's long past five.'

'Five?' she asked in surprise.

'You always returned at five', I said.

'Oh!' she recalled, as though I spoke of some prehistoric time.

'Were you in London all these days?' she asked.

'I've found a job. And that kept me away. How is Greta?'

She hesitated, a tiny moment's hesitation which had no significance, but in the evening haze it seemed sinister.

'I wanted to tell you, but I did not know where you lived.'

'Is she all right?'

'Yes, she's all right', she said swiftly, 'But she isn't here now. Her father came a few days back to fetch her. She's gone with him.'

I was looking at her. Everything within me ground to a halt. I was within it, within that stillness, and the world stood without. I had never seen the outside with such clarity.

'When was that?'

'The day you took her to Trafalgar Square. He came the day after that . . . you know he's found a job there.'

'And you?' I asked. 'you'll live here all alone?'

'I haven't made up my mind yet.' She lifted her head, her voice quivered, and momentarily I caught a glimpse of the girl in her face: the turned lips and wet eyes watching the pigeons flutter in the air.

'You must come to our house some day.' She wanted to take leave and I stretched out my hand. I followed her with my eyes for a long distance. Then I sat down on the bench. I had nowhere to go, nor reason to wait. Slowly the stars appeared over the trees. It was the first time I'd seen so many stars in the London sky, calm and bright, as if the rains had washed them too.

'It is time dear!'

The watchman of the park called out from a distance. He was going around the park, clattering the keys of the gate, checking under each tree, bush and bench with his torch for stragglers—a lost child, a drunkard, or a domestic cat.

There was no one there. Nothing had been left behind. I got up and moved towards the gate. Suddenly the wind picked up. A light breeze strayed into the darkness and the trees rustled. And then I heard a feeble voice, full of insistence. 'Stop . . . stop.' My feet came to a sudden halt in the middle of the park. I looked about. No one. No sound. No warning . . . only the trees swayed in the wind. I was overcome by an almost frenzied, desperate urge to sit there, amidst the trees where I had been caught the first time. I did not wish to go any further. I wanted to be caught, finally and irrevocably.

'It is closing time!' the watchman called, coming closer. He looked curiously at me, wondering if I was the man who had been sitting on the bench a while ago.

This time I did not turn, and breathed only after I had got out of the park. My throat was parched. It was nice to see the lantern of the pub opposite the park. I took out my wallet to count the money. The habits of penury die hard. I was astonished to see that I still had two pounds—until I remembered I had brought this much money for the pigeon-corn.

*Translated by Girdhar Rathi*

# Maya Darpan

Layers of burning sand had settled on the tin roof. When the wind rose a bright curtain of sand flapped around the house. The war-time barracks were being demolished, there were mounds of rubble every-where and it looked like the dust road had developed lumpy warts.

One could see everything from the window. Col-oured shadows slid across over the hillocks all day long. In the distance one heard, continuously, the sound of the stone-breaking machine. Like a growl-ing giant, *grr, grr, grr*.

Noises came and swept against the brittle edges of afternoon sleep. Taran woke up with a start. She touched her forehead. Strands of hair were sticking to her brow, the powder of her *bindi* had trickled down to the bridge of her nose. I have been awake all this while, she thought: it seemed to her she had been thinking the same thought while she was asleep . . . it's always like that in the afternoon—waves of sleep drift in and out of the eyes.

She washed her eyes, wiped off her *bindi*, worked the pump and splashed her face with water. From the bathroom window she could look out over the fields where they were pulling down the barracks. Half de-

molished, they stood around like broken-down
skeletons. The sand was ablaze. Taran could feel it
crackling between her teeth.

'Go and see Taran—if Babu is awake, take the *huk-
ka* to him', Bua called from the room adjoining the
kitchen. Even at her age Bua remembered everything. It seemed that while she did her chores, or
even sat dozing by the door, her attention was tugged
about by Babu's every need.

As soon as evening fell the Diwan Sahib waited for
his guests with impatient eagerness. Even if he went
out to the small rail station for a stroll he returned
hurriedly in the hope of some unexpected guest and
immediately asked Bua if someone had visited them
in his absence. She never said more than 'yes', 'no'.
After so many years she still had an unknown dread
of her brother. Even as a child she had kept her head
bowed before him. When she became a widow the
Diwan fixed on her a small pension. Now, in her dot-
age, she lived in his house. When Taran's mother
died the girl was left all alone. Had it not been for Bua
she could never have endured a moment in this dis-
mal place.

With sunset there was a regular little crowd in the
Diwan's verandah. The Government Supervisor, Mr
Das, the wealthy contractor, Meharchand, they all
came after their day's work and sat together for a
while. What was one to do, after all, in this wilderness; where could one enjoy an evening's pleasure? A
few tribal mud-huts, a couple of shacks selling *paan-
biri*, some wayside eating shops, and over there on
the hill the temple of Kali Devi. All said and done
there was just Diwan Sahib's house and these men

from different parts flocked to it eagerly.

'Taran, will you fill the *chillum* for Das Babu', the Diwan called, turning his face to the door. Now his veneer of indifference vanished. Das Babu had arrived, the others would be coming along. 'How is it you got so late today, the siren went off long ago', he said.

Das Babu had stuffed his round, flabby body into the chair. When he spoke his two rows of yellow teeth rattled faintly. 'I'd gone across the canal to see some land. On my way back I stopped at the new petrol pump. Now there won't be any petrol problem here Diwan Sahib.'

When Taran brought the *chillum* to him he shrank into himself. He was getting to be over fifty but he still felt nonplussed with a woman. Taran turned away and he relaxed, cleared his throat. Still, when he spoke there was strain in his voice: 'Why don't you make a trip to Haridwar, Rishikesh for a few days, Diwan Sahib? If nothing else it will be pleasant for your Bitia. She's alone all day long, doesn't she get bored?'

Das Babu would not call Taran by her name. If she had been a little younger he would not have felt this embarrassment. If she had been older the name could have been pronounced naturally. Between these two limits was raised an awkward constraint. Her youth seemed to have got stuck in the marsh somewhere . . . how was he supposed to regard her?

Diwan Sahib sat there, saying nothing in response. He enjoyed conversing with his friends, to be sure, but in his heart he always held himself aloof from them. There was a demarcated area of privacy which no one was allowed to cross.

Taran stopped short on hearing Das Babu's comment, then she went back inside. Bua was sitting there mending clothes. She avoided her and went into her own room. She shut the door and stood leaning against it for some time. The thick silence of the house pressed against her, the voices from the verandah were left floating out there, detached, unfamiliar, a little fearful.

From one of her windows she could see the verandah. If on an evening his friends did not turn up, Babu sat there alone with his eyes half-closed. How terribly remote he looked in his stillness! She had often thought—, I should go and sit with him, talk to him about this and that. After all there are only the two of us left; we can at least share each other's memories. But she had never taken the step. She just watched him from the window.

There was a strong wind those days. Gusts of hot dust came swirling upto the house, knocked about at the doors and then scattered in the courtyards. Far out in the distance they were dynamiting the boulders. Every now and then there was an explosion, then a vast echo. The earth under one's feet vibrated. And one could see flags fluttering a warning all over the landscape.

Taran sat dozing by the window. Then she suddenly got up, startled, as though someone had come and touched her. The twilight glow had spread across the fields and crept quietly upto her.

Bua came into the room and seeing her sitting in the dark admonished her: 'How many times I've told you, don't sit inside at this evening hour. Why don't you go out for a bit, you can take Shambhu along.'

But just then someone came climbing up the stairs. Taran looked out excitedly. Engineer Babu had arrived. How strange he is, she thought, he comes up thumping his feet and shakes up the whole house!

He had come to the township four or five months ago as a government architect, but everyone always called him Engineer Babu. He had simple, easy ways, and he talked in such a friendly manner—one would have thought he had lived in the place for years. He was not one of the regular visitors to the house. It was difficult to say if he could be called Babu's friend at all. Babu was twice his age and felt a little awkward in his company.

Taran went to the mirror and quickly tidied her hair, combing it down, waving it here and there. She powdered her face and her eyes fluttered. As she raised her hand to put on a *bindi*, below the parting of her hair, right in the middle of her forehead, she stopped and asked herself if this was some sort of a delusion. No, she did not delude herself any more. She was not attractive: this hardly even depressed her now. Years ago if someone looked her up and down in the street her whole body would start to flush and quiver. She would run back to her room and gaze at herself in the mirror for hours. What is it people notice in me . . . this question would tantalize her and she would think of answers with a panting heart. Now if anyone even glanced at her she felt a wry sort of surprise, and stepping out of herself she would look at her own body with careless inquisitiveness.

'And you are here, all by yourself at this hour?' Taran was interrupted. Engineer Babu stood at the door.

'I was just coming out to the verandah, have you had some tea?'

'I'll have tea another time. Some day when you agree to sit with us out on the verandah. I have to hurry off now.'

But Taran insisted that he stay for a bit. 'Wait, you must have something to eat. You've only just come', and she started off for the kitchen.

'No really, don't bother, please . . . I'm just on my way home from town and I've swallowed so much dust my stomach is all filled up.'

When he laughed Taran always felt a little wistful. Everyone in the township addressed him respectfully as Engineer Babu, yet he looked so young, even younger than herself. The first time she saw him sitting with her father's friends she was amazed. He looked like a college student among all those venerable men.

'You haven't come over that side again? Montu often asks after you.' Montu was his little servant. Every time Taran went for a walk along the railway line he would come and greet her.

'I'll come one of these days, will you be there?'

'Come next week, I have a load of work to get through in the next four or five days.'

Before leaving he stopped, took out his handkerchief and wiped his glasses. Taran raised her eyes and looked at him timorously, and her gaze hung on the spot even when he had moved away. What a man is Engineer Babu, she whispered to herself. When he pounds up the stairs the whole house trembles!

The dying sun had left a blood red trail across the sky. It was beginning to get dark. She could just make out the labourers' shacks huddled in between the boulders, and further away, on top of the hill, the temple of Kali, wrapped in a cloud of smoke.

She left the window and came to her bed. A half-written letter lay under her pillow. Every time she began writing to her brother his face emerged and hovered above the grey mass of time. Not the face he wore when he left home after quarelling with father. That was a distorted face, and even now her heart winced as she recalled it. No, not that face, but the one that looked on, young and so forlorn, when their mother died . . . She had looked up to him for consolation, not daring to cry before Babu, and he had whispered to her, 'Don't you see Taran, how lonely Babu is now? We must stay beside him. In a few days everything will be normal again.'

And did it ever become 'normal' again? She was very young then, she had not understood why her brother left home, why Babu had not been able to stop him. She knew now. Mother had been the only link between Babu and the rest of them. When she died each one fell apart and drifted away.

Bua came to call her for dinner. She looked at the paper in Taran's hand and asked, 'why, was there a letter?'

'I was writing to Bhai. His letter came yesterday.'

'He's asked you to come, has he?'

'Yes he's been asking me to come and spend some time with him. Bua, tell me, shall I go?'

Bua looked at her in amazement—all the way to Assam? She could not imagine Taran going so far away, and all alone. 'Ah, but if he feels so lovingly towards his sister why hasn't he come and met her during all these years? He has a quarrel with the father, but should he cut you off as well?'

Bua suffered from asthma, she could not speak for too long. She brought up a few words and the others drowned in her rising breath. Taran looked at the tears in her eyes and couldn't decide whether they were for her estranged brother or were squeezed out by the fit of coughing?

'You go along Bua, I'm just coming', she said casually.

A dull silence filled her room. She could hear the echo of her father's footsteps going up and down in the verandah. Outside there was pale moonlight and the mounds of rubble threw long, thin shadows across the empty fields.

A hazy image formed within her. Tea plantations . . . lush green spreading all over, up and down the sloping valleys . . . Somewhere there hidden inside a grove of trees is my brother's house, she thought. They say you have to go aboard a steamer to get there . . . wonder how it feels to travel on a steamer!

Taran stood and looked at the green signal beside the railway station. The wheels of the train rumbled close by the house, the hillocks all around and the distant boulders reverberated with the sound. For a while the frightful *grr grr* of the stone-breaking machine was drowned. The beam from the engine lit dry shrubs along the tracks. Then again a flickering hush shrouded everything.

That night Bua came and sat in Taran's room. She kept chopping betel-nut for herself. Every few minutes she gazed up at Taran and let out a long sigh, 'Are you asleep Taran?' she would ask in a doubting tone.

'No Bua, not yet.' Taran knew she was feeling her way to her. She lay there with her eyes closed, waiting.

'I went into your mother's room today', Bua started slowly. 'I was so amazed, Taran. How much she collected and preserved through the years. There was her wedding saree too, carefully folded and kept away in the big trunk.'

Curiosity stirred in Taran's heart. Once upon a time her own mother had been a bride. How difficult it was to imagine that.

'At that time your Babu had just been appointed Diwan . . . The wedding was such a grand affair. In the Muslim court he was the only Hindu Diwan but he had access to everyone.'

An irretrievable dream floated into Bua's eyes, the chopper lay still in her hand. 'One day the English Resident of the State came to meet him. Everyone in the locality came out and looked agog. But your Babu was so particular about his caste, as soon as the Englishman left he bathed himself clean and got the servants to throw away all the utensils.'

Taran sat up on her bed. How many times she had heard this story from Bua! Yet every time she felt a little thrill, as if each time she was being led anew into a strange illusory world.

'Bua, you've known Babu in those days, were you always so afraid of him?'

'Ah but who wasn't afraid of your father then? It's the same fear that continues to this day. Your mother was even more timid, she would just keep gazing up at him. He used to wear a dazzling white *chooridar*, a silk *achkan* and a superb pink turban . . . we couldn't take our eyes off him.' Bua's eyes travelled far out into the void and froze.

She continued, 'I keep wondering . . . When your Babu demands a high caste and a noble family as your match, is he justified? After all it's no longer the same. What *is* our status now that we should demand prestige? But then who will ever tell him this?'

Her face clouded over with bafflement, she couldn't work out how something long past and altogether finished could still cling to them like a leech. There were no honours attached to the family now, their properties had been sold and lost a long time ago. The house remained their one ancestral heritage. And of course the worn-out, dust-laden title of Diwan. You could wrap it around, flap it about, but it was immaterial. No one was likely to defer to it.

There was a lump in Bua's throat but a smile stuck to her face, as though she had forgotten to wipe it away. Taran did not like this part of Bua's ruminations. She liked to remember how her mother teased her, showing her what she was to take as her dowry. That used to tickle her, fill her with a lovely sensation . . . not the thought of her wedding, not even the jewellery . . . it was just an unknown happiness that welled up in her and she would float in it all alone.

Taran lay down again. She looked out of her window and at the signal, far out in the dark. Across the canal were the barracks. Night had sifted down upon them. Somewhere out there, she thought, in a narrow little room, Engineer Babu lives. She closed her eyes.

For a moment she became oblivious of herself. She

did not know whether Bua was still talking. A sweet weariness overcame her, that long-forgotten feeling welled up again and slipped down her legs. She was lying in a tub full of water, her body stretched out before her, soft and naked. Nothing had happened between then and now, whatever had been gained and lost with time was all present, drifting above the water's surface.

'Have you gone to sleep Taran?' Bua asked. Taran started, unclear whether she was on this or the other side of sleep . . . shadows flitted across over the water and she lay underneath in limpid silence.

Then there were days when the Diwan would not emerge from his room. The verandah would be deserted. The chairs stood around with dust. Bua would go to Babu's door and come back. He would ask for his food to be sent in to him. If he came out and encountered Taran he refused to look at her, and if he looked at her it would be as if he had trouble recognizing her. And he would turn away abruptly.

Taran had begun to understand why he unaccountably avoided her, why there was tension in the house. At first this had baffled and enraged her. But that time had gone by. Now a dry apathy filled her heart . . . why doesn't he get rid of me, she wondered. Bua had urged him many times to approach people. Letters were written, matters seemed to be taking shape. Her photograph and horoscope were sent off. But somehow everything always stopped midway. Taran couldn't understand why that happened.

Even now when Taran remembered that night her body shuddered . . .

Bua had come to her room just before midnight. She was awake, listening to Bua's footsteps coming towards her. She held her breath and kept lying.

Bua's voice was trembling. 'Did you hear something?'

Taran sat up in bed. 'What is it:'

'I can't stay in this house any longer.'

'What happened Bua?'

'Is there anything left to say Taran?' Her voice choked.

With numb heart Taran stared at the shadow in the dark that was Bua. 'He talked to you?'

'I was sitting in my room, he came himself . . . I ask you, if he has something to say why doesn't he say it direct to you? You aren't a baby any more, why on earth does he drag *me* into it?'

'But what did he say?'

'I can't figure him out. He started off saying it would have been best if it had all happened in your mother's lifetime. I used the opportunity and said— who goes by the family's name these days? It's more than enough if one can find a decent fellow. As soon as he heard this he stiffened. Then he strode out of the room and slammed the door. After a while when he came back I could hardly recognize him. His hair was dishevelled and his eyes were bloodshot. That's how he looked when your mother died, as if he wouldn't ever forgive her . . . He had a bundle under his arm. He came and threw it before me and said—Here's her mother's jewellery, she can take it all and go where she pleases. When her brother left home I didn't perish, did I? If *she* leaves nothing will happen either . . . I was quite bewildered. Taran. How can he talk like this about his own daughter?'

That night Bua's question hovered about her in the dark. She couldn't grasp what her father wanted of her. He had become suspicious of her—that she would escape him one day. Like her brother. She had never considered the possibility, but that night her father's dread became her own. She felt restless and then guilty. Did she really want to live on in this house? She asked herself this again and again, and she realized that Babu was right. She had a horror of the house, the empty rooms. She tried deluding herself but the question nagged her—do you want to go on living here?

Such a simple question and she wouldn't dare answer it. All night she crouched in her bed, her face hidden in the pillow, quailing before her own dreams.

Then, one day, she suddenly decided she would visit her brother for a few days. But she could not bring herself to tell Babu. She went to his room several times and turned back. Finally, she asked Bua to go and tell him. Bua gazed at her doubtfully but later when she thought it over it seemed a good idea to let her go away for a while.

That day Babu called her to his room. She went and stood hesitantly at his door. Her breath caught in her throat, she felt stifled.

'Come in and sit here', Babu said in a dull voice. He sat resting on a pillow against the wall, very quiet and very still. A thought flashed in her mind—there is still time, I should turn and go back to my room, quietly, as I came, and it will all pass away . . . But her feet were suddenly glued to the floor.

'I believe you want to go away for a while?' Taran sat there, alert in her silence. She thought—he does not want to mention my brother, he never refers to him. Every time a letter came from him he would send it on to her without opening it.

'You don't feel happy here Taran?' There was bleak curiosity in his voice, and an innocence, as though he had thought of this as a possibility for the first time.

Taran looked up at him and her heart lurched. Maybe Babu will ask me to stay, she thought feverishly, maybe he also feels lonely without me. She began trembling all over. If only he would ask me to stay, she thought, I would immediately drop the idea of going . . . just let him ask me . . .

But Babu didn't say a word. Taran lowered her eyes.

'It's all right, if you want to go you can. Don't worry about me', he said finally. His voice was level, unfeeling.

Going out of the room she faltered a little. She hoped he would call her back, say something else. But the room was filled with a terrible silence.

That afternoon she lay in her room, willing herself to sleep. She would have liked to be able to draw sleep to herself any moment of the day, like a shroud. This compulsion to keep awake, to look around with wide open eyes, it seemed unnecessary and false. She had begun to wonder if all her waking moments all these years had not been a sort of delusion . . . they had hovered about at sleep's edge and left her untouched.

In the evening Taran came out of her room. Her

body dragged because of the day's lethargy. The wind had blown all day. The sky was lined with thick yellow layers of sand. Far off, the sun glittered on rocks. Taran noticed that Babu had not come out to the verandah, his door was still shut.

Bua sat in her own room, coughing and mumbling something to herself. Every time the breeze swept through the house all the doors rattled. Taran went back to her room quickly and put on her sandals. She told Bua she was going out for a walk. But she couldn't tell if Bua had heard her at all; she could hear her gurgling cough as she descended the steps.

The sand fields stretched out to the far horizon. The sun had left a mottled layer of gold on the ground. Beside the new road, rubble heaps stood about like pyramids. Taran walked along these and reached the water tank.

She was very familiar with this barren landscape, had been witness to its modulations ever since she was a child. During wartime when the barracks were being erected a whole lot of military trucks would drive around, rashly raising clouds of dust. She was there then . . . now, when those giant boulders were being cut down to make a new road and the barracks stood aside half demolished, she was there again, watching everything from her window, all day long.

But soon she was going to be rid of all this, she thought with a little tremor. And when she saw Engineer Babu coming down the road she broke into a smile.

He came and stopped by the water tank. His shirt sleeves were rolled up and she could see his hairy forearms coated with dust. There was sweat on his neck, all along the open shirt collar. His eyes were always alert behind his glasses, restless and yet extremely serious.

'How come you're standing here?'

'Oh, I'd come out for a stroll. It's so close in the house, I couldn't bear it . . . I saw you from a distance, Engineer Babu, though I could hardly recognize you in that sola topee.'

He laughed and Taran remembered the first time she had heard that laugh. She had hidden herself behind the door of the verandah where Babu entertained his friends and she had watched him, saying to herself—he is even younger than I am . . .

'Have you been to the town, Engineer Babu?'

'No, how could I?' He recounted his problems with such style, one would have thought he quite relished them. 'How could I? The lorry has not been out for three days. I can't get there on my own, nor can Montu.'

'The lorry hasn't been? But who brings the food then? There isn't even a decent restaurant here.'

'Ah but you don't know Montu', he laughed boyishly. 'We are both lazy about going shopping into town, so he's discovered a nice *dhaba* here. He gets food for us both from there.'

Taran gazed at him in wonder. What a man is Engineer Babu, she thought. He's come all the way here, leaving behind his home and family. And there is no one here in this wilderness he can call his own, except his little servant.

'Come you'd set out for a stroll, let's go on.' They started walking on the rough, uneven path. Every time the wind blew against them they had to swallow a mouthful of dust. In the Kali temple right above the labourers' hovels the evening lamp had been lit. A white curtain of sand fluttered around it, screening it from the last rays of the sun gliding about on the slope of the hill.

Engineer Babu stopped suddenly. 'Do you see the boulders behind those huts?' His gaze went and rested far off. Taran looked at him curiously. 'After the road is made all those will be razed to the ground. The land around the railway line will be prepared for cultivation. On the far side of the canal factories will come up. You'll see everything change before your eyes.'

His voice had become eager. The glass of his spectacles glinted in the evening sun. He always related such exciting stories. And Taran gazed at him fascinated, thinking to herself—he looks just like a college boy, yet how much he knows. But one detail always made her laugh. He spoke to her so vehemently of his plans, almost as if she were going to thwart them!

They stopped at the gate beside the railway line. He had become silent now, as if the gathering dusk had hushed him and left him suddenly forlorn. A slender moon lit the sky. The jagged cliffs which looked harsh in daylight seemed to soften in the evening glow. They lost their aggressive bulk and huddled closer to each other.

'Engineer Babu, have you ever been in Assam?'

'Assam, no, why, what's there?'

'Nothing, I just thought of it. My brother lives there. He's about your age.'

'Oh', he said, a little uninterested, and she felt

embarrassed. The wind had fallen, it was almost night. She had to turn back from here.

'Perhaps you should return home now. It's getting late. Shall I send Montu with you?'

'No I will go on my own, its hardly any distance.'

He crossed the rail tracks and started walking across the vast, bare fields. Taran turned round and kept looking after his receding figure. Then she started walking back and an inexpressible happiness rose inside her . . . All the nagging worries seemed irrelevant, she could not explain to herself why she had been afraid for so long, what after all had made her so afraid? Now look at Engineer Babu, she said to herself, here he is, so far away from his home, what must he feel? And walking across the dust road she felt as if all the staleness of the past years had been washed away from her. No, now I will never return to this house, she repeated to herself, I shall live my own life, I will not let anyone drag me back into this wasteland.

Climbing the steps of her house Taran noticed the verandah was deserted; the whole house stood in absolute silence. There was light only in the kitchen and it stretched out in a faded patch upto Babu's door.

The door was slightly ajar. Taran began to feel uneasy—was Babu sitting there all by himself in the dark room? She came up to the room and pushed open the door a little further. Now her hands were trembling. At first she could not make out anything in the dark. Her eyes kept hunting about in the room. Then, suddenly, she shrank back. Yes, Babu was there, walking about in the room as if in a delirium. She watched him. He suddenly stopped in the middle of the room, as if trying to capture a forgotten memory. Then, as abruptly, he turned round and walked up to the photograph that had stood for years in the little alcove. She saw him take it up and wipe off the dust with his unsure hands . . . An image gleamed through the faded curtain of memories. The photograph was taken at the silver jubilee celebrations of George the Fifth. Babu sat there, amidst other state officials, flanking the English Resident . . . He stood there with the image in his hand, hypnotized to see himself *there*, sitting with them in such glory.

Taran came in and stood by the door, petrified. This was the first time she had seen an old man so nakedly. Babu's dry grey hair, his bony hands with the blue veins sticking out, all those innumerable wrinkles which made his face so pitiable . . . he had grown old before her very eyes.

'Babu', Taran's lips fluttered. She came and stood before him in the darkness. This was perhaps the first time she had dared to go so close to him.

He raised his head and looked at her. There was a glaze over his eyes. 'What have you come for?' he asked tremulously.

She turned and came out of the room, then stood for a long time in the verandah outside. A fear began to crawl about in her mind . . . Babu will never let me go, she thought, I will live here alone, bound to his shadow . . . Even when he is gone his wretchedness will always, all my life, cling to me . . .

The moment of courage that had come and touched her that evening was fled already. Perhaps it had never belonged to her . . . no, it would not return to her again.

All night she could hear Bua coughing in her room. Sometime in the middle of the night Taran went to Babu's room and stood there, leaning against the door. She felt as if her mother had died again that night and that she was weeping away the tears that had remained choked within her all those years.

Then she came back to her room and stood by the open window. There was moonlight over the arid fields. A few lights twinkled beyond the railway line. Engineer Babu lives somewhere there, she thought. And suddenly she remembered what he had said to her, that in a few years everything would change. Was he right? She smiled now, a dry, wan smile.

She came away from the window and lay on the bed. Her eyes were heavy but she could not sleep for a long time. Once she was swept by a light wave of sleep and dreamt her brother stood before her. That dear, familiar face with its lonely eyes . . . It was so long ago that she had seen him, would she know him now if she ever chanced upon him, all of a sudden?

And then it all came floating before her eyes . . . Somewhere very far away, hidden in the shades of a plantation, her brother's house. They say you have to go aboard a steamer to get there . . . wonder how it feels to travel on a steamer!

*Translated by Geeta Kapur*

# Exile

I heard someone shout my name and, surprised, I stopped right there in the middle of the busy street and saw a woman, faintly familiar, run up to me.

She came to a stop opposite me. She was short of breath. If the memory of a closed room is prised open in a wide open space, with the crowds milling around and all the noise, one cannot but be taken aback. I had seen her only once before, in her house. She was wearing a sari then. Now she was in a skirt; a shopping bag was slung over her shoulder, a scarf held down her hair. Her face was clear and white in the high sun—and impassive.

Without saying a word she led me by my hand—she almost dragged me—to the kerb.

'I've been twice to your room but found it locked both times.' She took a handkerchief from her handbag and wiped the sweat off her forehead.

When a man is thus trapped he talks at great length, partly to get over his feeling of embarrassment and partly to gain time to find a way out. So I recounted to her in unnecessary detail impressions of my journeys and the cities I had visited, not realizing she was staring hard at me all the while and paying little attention to what I was saying. Indeed, she was not listening at all.

My indifference towards her, bordering on dislike, rose to the surface.

'Your children—are they well?' I had thought of them on the spur of the moment.

She forced a smile to her lips.

'I'm being a bother to you', she said, dabbing the handkerchief on her forehead again, not so much to mop the sweat away as the anxiety. 'You see, there are some letters from Calcutta, all in Bengali, and I can't read a word of them'. She began to fumble with the catch of her handbag.

I put my hand on hers. 'Look, can't it wait?' I said. 'I'll come around one of these days.'

She raised her eyes. Two moist fragments of the sun peeped out of them. Neither self pity nor sorrow, just a hint of bewilderment in those two eyes as they fastened on me.

'Will you—really?'

Suddenly I wanted to reassure her, get it over with quickly and cleanly and get lost. But the crowd and the noise dissipated the sentiment.

Then she left. Soon her face faded within the anonymity of the crowd. But the grey scarf about her grizzled head, the bag hanging from her shoulder, her outmoded skirt below the knees—these have stuck in my memory. There are some people whose faces cannot be recalled, only their clothes. Their face is only a reflection held in the mirror of their apparel.

I remember the day I met her for the first time.

It was a different day altogether. I had been in the city only a short time, lonely and alone. Loneliness can be bad enough the first few days in a foreign country, but those were late autumn days when even shadows wilted to a depressing yellow. Tired of sitting on the benches by the river all day long, I would often seek refuge in one of the concert halls. I did not much care for Bach and Mozart then, but it did take my mind off the cold unfriendly streets. I would carefully choose my seat in the hall so as not to be a nuisance if I fell asleep during the performance.

I cannot recollect the music now, nor perhaps does it matter, but on one of those evenings I went to the restaurant attached to the concert hall for a coffee during the intermission. It was crowded and a long queue stood to the counter. So I made my way out to the foyer. It was colder, but there were very few people there.

I did not know I was being watched as I stood looking out through the tall plate-glass window at the fading light. Beyond was the river, lost in the gathering darkness. But I knew it was there all right.

Suddenly I felt a hand on my shoulder. 'Listen',— he spoke even before I could turn round—'aren't you an Indian?'

To this day his words hang in the air in their abject eagerness.

'I'm not sure I can place you.' I looked at him uncertainly. He was a very short, lean man, rather dark, with sharp features and no trace of embarrassment.

'I can't either', he said, smiling. 'But it isn't everyday you come across an Indian here! I couldn't believe it when I saw you.'

He ran his eyes over me, trying to size me up. But evidently he was out of his depth. His eyes neither disturbed nor attracted me. His pensive smile, though, exuded a smouldering warmth which took me back to my country.

'You come here often?' I asked.

'I used to. You know, in the beginning every Indian who comes out here for the first time goes about like a hungry wolf!' He laughed mirthlessly, but it did show he wanted to come closer.

'Have you been here long?'

'Nine years', he said, looking away, his interest in me suddenly on the wane. Then in a strange distant voice: 'You don't mind, do you? I've no business to butt in on you like this.'

I tried to assure him that it was a pleasure.

'It looks like you're a newcomer, aren't you?'

It felt odd to be thus labelled but obviously he had not meant it as a dig—at least I did not think so. He would have gone on talking—he had that famished look—but the bell went in the hall.

'See you after the concert. I'll be up here.'

With that he turned round to join the rush at the door. I stayed behind in the deserted foyer to finish my cigarette. Some people do thrust themselves on you, but I could not, in all fairness, say this of him. Still, his manner had a certain persistence which made me restless. Back in my seat in the hall I could not stop thinking of him. And certainly that did not make me look forward to seeing him again.

But when I came out after the concert I saw him waiting near the exit, standing apart from the stream of people. He smiled at me and fell into step beside me without a word.

We emerged into the street. It led straight to the

tram stand. I did not mind his tagging along. We walked on in the dark. It was very cold and quiet under the trees. No breeze rustled in the treetops, nor did leaves from the bare branches nearby come loose and fall to scatter the silence.

'You're shacking up alone?'

'Yes.'

'Well you don't have to be in a hurry then!' he said, relieved, as if we were old friends seeing each other after years, with the whole night before us.

'So this is your first autumn out here?'

'Yes.'

'How different and strange it can all be! Back home you know one never really knows when the trees shed leaves and put out new ones. But here it's almost like an avalanche. In the beginning it used to make me feel terrible.'

'It's certainly been a long time', I said. 'Couldn't you go back home?'

He was silent for only a short moment but in that darkness it seemed as if he had not spoken a long time. Then abruptly he pulled up, right there on the pavement, as if the stream of his thoughts had run dead into a hurdle.

'You tell me! Is it easy to go back?'

I had stopped too. I wished I could see the look on his face but the darkness gave away nothing.

'There's an old pub nearby. I don't drink but maybe you'd care to peep in', he said, in a bid to sound me out.

I was immediately grateful, not being in any particular hurry to get back to my apartment and rather put out by this walk in the cold. I no longer resented his company: after a time one learns to insulate one-self against the presence of others.

He turned into an alley. I followed him. His easy and confident stride suggested he knew his city well. But when he stopped in front of a run-down building I began to have doubts about his judgement. He turned to me. 'It's an old place', he said. 'They brew their own beer. They've been in business since some-time in the eighteenth century. I come here often.'

He was right. As we went in it looked like a home-coming. All the waiters and regulars knew him well. While he exchanged small talk with them I looked round the pub. Lion and tiger heads glared down from the walls. The beams under the roof were black with soot. Over the counter hung a smudged and cracked picture of the Madonna.

He was beaming when he returned to our table. 'They're all my friends. I've known them for years.' The diffidence which marked his face at the concert hall had given way to confidence; he looked com-pletely transformed.

He ordered beer for me and tea and lemon for him-self. I was rather surprised for he did not look the man to spurn a drink.

'You come here for—this?' I said, laughing.

'But of course, no!' he said. 'Not until my doctors refused to oblige me. But I still come here once in a while. Habits die hard you know.'

The pub had subdued lighting, enough to throw his features into relief. He must have had a soft, smooth complexion, once. Now it was all rough and coarse, although his eyes were still deep and sensitive. His eyebrows were thick and bushy, balancing as it were the brown geometric planes on either side. But right now they merely looked like so much weight over his eyes.

'Sure you won't join me?' To drink alone can be quite trying; it certainly is little short of torture in the company of the abstemious.

'The doctors say I can drink but at my own risk.' He laughed aloud. 'As if earlier they'd been running the risk!'

I did not insist. But it aroused my interest to know that he had been in a hospital. For a whole year, he told me. He had fallen ill soon after coming here from Calcutta. It was his lungs. He was sent to a sanatorium and later to many hospitals. 'I could only get away from there with great difficulty', he said nonchalantly, but guilt appeared in the lines of his face.

The restlessness I had felt in the concert hall began to recede. He was no longer a stranger, only a man on the outside come back from the other-worldly atmosphere of hospitals. Perhaps people who have spent lonely days in a sanatorium, a jail or even in the mountains, are pursued by a shadow: they are marked for life.

He smiled warmly at me and I glimpsed a disturbing sorrow, a quiet suffering in his eyes.

'I'm better now', he said reassuringly. 'Had I been in Calcutta I'd have kicked the bucket long ago.'

'Was there much pain?'

'Pain?' He repeated the word slowly. Some words, so commonplace, become suddenly transparent on the lips of another man: you can see in them the entire outline of a life. I felt small before the enormity of the word I had used.

'No, I've been lucky', he said. 'I met a woman in the hospital. She used to work there. I owe my life to her. And now . . .', he hesitated a moment, 'she is my wife. I was the first Indian she'd ever met . . . Don't you think it's kind of funny?'

'No, I don't think so.' It was my second beer and I was slowly entering that plane of muted consciousness where either everything or nothing is funny. I was pleasantly surprised to hear that he was not all that alone, he had hearth and home.

'You must be a little puzzled, though.'

'What about?'

'Well, for one, I'm sitting here with you till so late in the night.' He stopped, acutely embarrassed. 'It's become impossible to stay home ever since I last got back from the hospital. Back in India it might have been different. Here I just don't know what to do.'

'Why don't you go back home?' I asked, lifted on the surge of courage which comes only when you are slightly high.

'Which home?' Fear stared out of his eyes. 'I didn't get you.'

He was so close that I recoiled. Sometimes one can smell fear, elemental, animal fear. The mist lifts from it and one may follow its scent to the dark den of the soul where every move is a gamble. But I stopped in my tracks as though he had inadvertently shown me his cards. I looked away.

'Would you care for another drink?' His tone became very formal. He may have seen me beat a retreat.

'No', I said. 'It's time we hit the road now.' I stood up. He paid the bill. We walked out.

Outside the deserted lane was submerged in silence. The shops had closed for the night. Their neon
lights, left on, picked up the litter in the lane. Some
drunks lay on the square steps, cackling.

We turned towards the main road. I was very cold
and in a hurry to reach the tram stand. He was still
lost in brooding silence and I could hear his heavy
breathing. Our footsteps echoed in the dark empty
lane. It was rather frightening.

He stopped at the last bend in the lane.

'You sure you want to go to your room at this late
hour?' he asked, trying to sound casual.

'Well?'

'We live close by.'

I would not take his hint.

'She must be home. Don't you want to see her?'

'At this time?'

'Well, it's at this time she gets back from the hospital. She'll be very happy to meet you.'

His insistence was almost morbidly disquieting, as
though I would imperil his life *and* mine by walking
away and leaving him alone in the darkness.

'I'll come over some other time—when she has her
day off.'

He merely stared at me.

'You'll remember the address, won't you?'

'Sure I will.'

I was not so sure though. All that I had wanted
then was to be rid of him.

But I could not have steered clear of him for long. I
should have known that very night that I would visit
him sooner or later. So, one day, I found myself at his

place, and rather early in the afternoon too. I had taken it for granted that it would take some time to look about for the house; but, quite the contrary, I walked straight up to it. It lay between the square and the river. The noise of the streets I had passed through seemed abruptly truncated. And right there, near the mouth of the maimed stump, in an island of silence, stood his house.

I would perhaps have overlooked it had I not seen two children—a girl and a boy—playing in the sun. The girl must not have been more than six or seven years old. The boy, who was the younger of the two, sat with his back to me. As I spoke her father's name she stayed her hand in mid-play. She regarded me with intense curiosity. She pointed towards the door without a word and until I went in I could feel her eyes fastened on my back.

Whenever I recall that day I see a wan autumn sun, I see two children playing near the square steps, and I feel again a pair of eyes fixed on me.

I rang the bell. The door gave on an empty room. I could see nobody inside—not even whoever opened the door. There was but a stale odour that pervades houses which remain shut for much of the time—an odour that the household grows used to but which assails a visitor as he steps in.

'Excuse me, I'll just be a moment!'

It was a woman's voice coming from an inner room. I could not see the woman, but her voice started me on the way to knowing her.

I did not sit down for to make room to sit I would have had to shift the things which lay all over the place. There were children's books on the couch, clothes on the chairs, sweepings in an ungathered heap on the floor. I had come much before my time.

'He should be home any time now. He told me all about you', she said, coming into the room. She was short of breath although she had only walked across a room or two.

'Am I too early?'

'No, no! But he should have been back sooner. It gets dark early these days.'

'Has he gone out somewhere?'

'He must be on his way . . . You didn't have difficulty in finding the house, did you?' She wore an agitated look and it seemed to be a permanent feature of her face. She cast an embarrassed eye on me and on the things lying around . . . She looked a stranger in her own house.

When I now turn back to that day I find I cannot see her face as I saw it then. I thought she looked so incongruous: her sari was an almost-cheap loud pink and did not go with either her agitated look or with the formality of my visit. The suspicion that she had put on a sari only for my benefit made me shrink in my own estimation.

'You came from India lately, didn't you?'

'A month back. I ran into your husband sometime then. I know nobody else here.'

'Oh him!' For a moment her face became strained, then it dissolved in laughter. 'He brings home all the Indians he can get hold of!'

There was a hint of sarcasm in her tone—not aimed at me in particular but at the whole situation of which I was only a part. Her intent eyes lingered on me a fraction of a moment too long, secretly assigning me my place among the Indians her husband brought home.

'They're your children out there?'

'Which children?' She threw me a suspicious, un-comprehending glance.

'They're playing outside. The girl pointed out the house to me.'

'Oh she must be Aparna—with her brother', she said offhandedly, as if talking of somebody else's children.

'Would you care for some tea or . . .?'

'No. Let him come.'

'Do you know when he'll be back?'

I looked up at her sharply, taken aback. 'No! In fact I'd expected he'd be home.'

'Well he should have been but he isn't!' She gave a low, sardonic chuckle. 'Come, how much did he tell you? He was with you a long time the other night.' Her eyes now fastened on me. It struck me that she was a woman of mature years. She had dark lines under eyes etched by lifelong grievances.

'We met only once.'

'Once is enough! He tells everyone', she said wearily. 'So I thought he must have told you too.'

'What about? His illness?'

'Yes, that too . . . Didn't he tell you about going back home to India?' She fixed an intent gaze on me to see if I was keeping from her what she knew for sure in her heart and feared and still wanted to hear from me. But I did not know what it was.

'Didn't he really tell you anything of the sort?' Her fear reached out to lay its cold finger on me.

'No—believe me he didn't. He didn't mention it at all.'

A precarious, twilight silence settled between us. When at last the voices of children raised in play filtered in she almost jumped out of her chair.

'Oh look how dark it has become!'

She switched on the light. Earlier the gathering darkness had somehow brought us close to each other. Now the glare of the light made us strangers again. She left the room.

I was seized with a desire to walk out. She wouldn't even know, I told myself. But at the same time I realized I would despise myself later if I took the impulse. It would have seemed so cowardly, sneaking out like a thief. So I forced myself to keep sitting.

Silence descended on the house. A breeze struck up outside and the calendar on the wall fluttered. The radiant faces of the divine couple, Shiva and Parvati, looked benignly down from it. On the mantlepiece lay a packet of joss sticks beside a picture of the Kali Ghat. The shelf had Bengali books arrayed on it. Wherever the eye fell something or the other Indian could be seen. In a foreign country she seemed to be too much of an Indian. A *tanpura* stood in a corner, a film of dust on it. It had not been touched for a long time.

When the outer door creaked open I saw him framed in the doorway. He looked much the same as in the foyer of the concert hall. He was wearing the same clothes, which looked neither new nor dirty.

'Have you been waiting long? Where is she?'

'She's just gone in.'

'So you've already met her', he said, throwing me a cursory glance. He removed the bags from his shoulders and put them in a corner. 'You aren't bored, are you? Did you like her?'

'Who?' I asked absentmindedly.

'My wife, who else! She likes to meet my Indian friends.'

His eyes acquired the sheen and penetration of the same suspicion and fear which I had seen earlier in his wife's eyes.

'She's never been to India you know.'

The silence that followed resounded with the fluttering of the calendar on the wall.

A little later both the children came in. The boy made straight for the kitchen but the girl stopped to look in, surprised that her father should be home so early in the evening.

'Come on!' He drew her close to him. 'Tell him your name.'

'Aparna', she mumbled shyly, but I didn't get it. She repeated it still more shyly.

'Do you know Bengali?' I asked her. She stared blankly at me.

'No she doesn't.' He pulled her closer. 'I was in the hospital when she was small. Later somehow I could never find time to teach her.'

She was a brown-skinned girl but looked fairer in the pale electric light. Her hair and eyebrows had taken after her father's. Her eyes and chin reflected a hardiness reminiscent of her mother.

'Say something or he'll think you're a dumb girl!' His fingers gently smoothed back her hair. Still she did not speak; she only batted her eyes, taking us in.

I took her hand. She let it rest in my grasp.

'I've very much wanted to take them to Calcutta.' His hands still moved on his daughter's head as if of their own accord. He had a distant look in his eyes.

'Then why don't you? You've been here a long time now.'

'I make up my mind to every year. But we've had to put it off for some reason or the other.'

'Do they want to go very much?'

'They're crazy about going!' He laughed. 'They look forward to it every year, both mother and children, as if they belonged there.'

The girl's hand lay numb in mine. I do not know if she understood our talk. She may not even have been listening. She merely held her father in a steady gaze.

When we heard his wife call out for us we trooped out to the dining room. It was a smaller room but looked spacious in the absence of table and chairs. We squatted on a mat.

She brought in the dishes. She still had a forlorn air about her but was no longer agitated. At work in her kitchen, with those beads of sweat on her forehead, she looked familiar enough and attractive. This I would not have known had I not seen her daughter from such proximity. One is so accustomed to seeing the image of parents in their children that when one sees a reflection of children in parents one is taken aback.

'You cooked all this?'

She laughed to see me surprised. 'He taught me!' There was heaps of food—fried rice, fish curry, mint chutney and so on. It was a long time since I had eaten Indian food.

The children sat one on either side of their father. It seemed they were closer to him than to their mother—probably because he spent most of his time outdoors.

'They've only each other to play with', she remarked suddenly, looking at her children. 'I complained to their teacher but nobody bothers.'

'But why should you complain to the teacher', I asked.

'The schoolboys make fun of them. They call them gypsies.' She laughed to take the sting out of it. 'They call anyone a gypsy if the colour of his skin is so much as a shade darker. So no one talks to our children. No one plays with them.'

'You're very touchy', he said. 'Don't you remember how people would stare at me when I first came over here?'

'It's different with you. Children are more sensitive; they take it to heart.' She looked to me for support. 'Had we been in Calcutta they wouldn't have had to go through this.'

'You keep hammering away at it!' His voice had an edge of irritation, the helpless kind—as if they had gone over this many times before.

The children ate unconcernedly.

We lapsed into silence. No one spoke while eating. Not even when he poured us white wine which he had brought with him from the market. After we had eaten she left with the boy to put him to bed. The girl remained sitting, her head on her father's shoulder.

'Would you like to listen to some songs?' he asked me uncertainly.

'Sure, I'd love to!' I had ceased to be surprised: I

had begun to expect almost anything in the house.

He whispered something to his daughter. She left the room quietly and returned with the *tanpura* and a small notebook wrapped in red cloth—the way Rajasthan traders wrap their account books. The father and daughter smiled at each other, silently sharing a common secret.

For the first time in the evening I saw a smile part the girl's lips.

Then she shuffled a little backwards on the floor and he a little forwards. The *tanpura* in one hand, he turned over the pages of the notebook with the other. He cast a glance at the door. Silence crept over us— the restless stillness which, broken, leaves a scar.

The scar is still on me though I cannot put my finger on it. It was a Tagore song he was singing. The girl sat huddled behind him. His eyes, intent on his fingers, moved with them as they glided on the string of the *tanpura*. Like those other disembodied shadows gliding across, resounding with the swish of autumn leaves as they fell and were blown about on the lazy breath of a southwester, which, here in our country, means so little, but which that evening while I sipped at my wine in a foreign country recalled to me the sounds and the languor of my leaking roof and brought me face to face with the spider that sways in the rain and the sun and the mist, spinning its gossamer web tirelessly round us somewhere deep within. My eyes followed his fingers on the *tanpura*. He faltered just for a fraction of a moment as his wife entered the room after having put the boy to bed. She walked across softly, careful not to make any noise, and sat in a corner.

He went on singing for a long time, looking up songs in his notebook, a half-smile on his lips.

We were so absorbed it surprised us when he finished. We waited, thinking there was more to come. But it didn't. At last the girl got up, smoothed the pages of the notebook and gently patted it shut, and stood the *tanpura* in a corner.

'Did I bore you?' he asked, looking at me.

'Had I been bored I'd have noticed the time long ago. Look how late it is already!' Indeed it had become very late. I wasn't even sure that I would catch the last tram. I turned to his wife to take leave of her and saw she was still sitting expectantly, all by herself, in a corner. The end-fold of her sari had fallen to the floor and she had covered her head with both her hands. I suspected that she, despite being a part of his family, was not with it; she was an outsider or a guest—as I was.

The girl stood leaning against the door. She joined the palms of her hands in salutation when her father asked her to. I was already at the outer door when her mother, suddenly coming to, called out to say: 'If you miss the tram you can come back for the night.' I nodded in assent. I could not then have foreseen the circumstances under which I would later call on them.

He walked with me to the tram stand. A mist had gathered over the treetops. The moon had risen, cold, distant, and very, very still. We walked on, keeping to ourselves.

'You've no regrets have you?' he asked.

'What for?'

'For calling on us.' His laugh was rather frightening, like the beating of bats' wings close by in the darkness, unseen, sending a chill down the spine.

We walked on fast. The streets were deserted. Nothing was heard except his heavy breathing and my own heavier footfalls.

'Listen', he said, 'You're very fortunate.'

'How come?' I laughed. I had never thought of myself in those terms.

'You can go back home any time you want.'

'Well it's not asking for much, is it?'

'No, no, don't say that! You don't know how much something like that means.' He came to a standstill and the streetlight fell full into his face. 'I haven't even spoken of this to anyone before but . . . Well, you know, some people are afraid of going back home. It's all right making plans for going but you get cold feet when the time comes to leave.'

I don't remember how long we stood there under the light in the deserted street. Perhaps he wanted to talk some more and would have—but for the clang of the approaching tram. The pavement shone in the passing light. We ran for the tram. At the stand we did not have time enough to say proper goodbyes. He was panting as he stood outside the carriage and I was panting inside.

I remembered that panting ever after.

Now I stood at his doorstep a second time. In the meantime the autumn cold and the spring sunshine had gone. The passage of seasons had left its imprint on me too, and the memory of those people had receded and blurred. Then during the long hot days of the summer I left on a tour of the European countries. When I returned I was very much a man of the world, a well-seasoned man who had learnt to keep his distance from other Indian novices. I was no longer a helpless expatriate. Although I still had a store of loneliness wrapped round me I was snug within its fold.

On my return I heard he was dead. The Indian community there was quite small and every birth and death was common knowledge before long. Rumour had it that one day he disappeared from his house and two days later the family heard from a hospital in another town that he was dead. It was anybody's guess what circumstances drove him to the hospital.

I would have ignored the rumour and forgotten all about it had she not run into me on the street. It was a purely chance meeting and I was surprised she had been to my house twice during my absence. It was all the more surprising that she had gone all the way to my place just so that I might read those letters for her.

The square looked much the same in the sunshine that it had the previous year. The trees had not begun shedding their leaves. The air had the tang of summer's end.

Both children were playing outside by themselves. I recalled what she'd told me: 'They've only each other to play with.' They stopped playing as they saw me. The boy stood up in his place. A flicker of recognition passed over the girl's face.

She got up, walked on very steady feet and passed by me without a word. I followed her. Our footsteps must have been heard inside for the door opened before either of us could knock.

She stood in the doorway, a long shadow trailing behind her. She had on the same sari, that loud eye-sore pink. On her forehead I saw for the first time a round vermilion spot. She wore some cheap vari-coloured glass bangles round her wrists. It all depressed me for no reason.

'Come on in, let's go to the terrace.'

We went up dark stairs and emerged onto a small terrace. It occupied but a corner of the roof, bound by a parapet in place of railings. Two chairs had already been put there. Perhaps she'd been waiting there for me and had seen me come down the street.

'You won't be cold here, will you?' She turned towards me.

'In this sun?' I laughed. 'I didn't know you had such a neat little terrace—so much like the ones we've got in India.'

'You like it?' she asked eagerly, lowering herself onto a footstool close to the chair I had dropped into. The stool was so low it disappeared behind the un-gainly folds of her sari. 'He was also very fond of it. Sometimes while I'd be looking for him all over the house he'd be quietly lazing here.'

'That must have been in the very early days?'

'Yes—till sometimes after we'd moved in. Later I got used to it.' She looked away towards the other rooftops and was silent.

I could almost see her step out of herself and with-draw to where the voices of her children fluttered in the square and rose to us.

'Would you care for a drink?' she asked.

'No—don't feel like it.' The voices of the children held me fast in spite of myself.

'Do they still have to play alone?'

'They have their holidays now—the time they wait for the year round.' Her voice, so remote and far away, reached me low but clear.

I raised my head. The sun had retreated from the square but still lingered on the rooftops.

'Have you told the children?' My words dragged at an old memory, like children dragging a dead sparrow in sport across the dust.

'No I haven't.' She was looking down at the square. 'They know nothing.'

They did not know! A shiver ran down inside me and curled itself up into a cold knot, and I recalled an evening long, long ago, like some painting in a museum, his fingertips frozen on the string of the *tanpura*, the staring eyes of a girl crouched behind him, and she who was now sitting in front of me in the dying sun, many, many evenings removed, in a corner, her head bent low: a picture frozen in the eternal frame of evening gloom.

'Haven't you really told them anything?' I asked her incredulously.

Her eyes regarded me for a long, silent moment. 'Why, what have you heard?'

'I?' I felt I had been caught red-handed. 'Very little indeed—only this, that one day he left the house and . . . '

'And never returned', she completed the sentence for me, although I could still see its loose end in mid-air.

'Didn't I tell you it's not good to get used to things? This I know now—I've taken long to learn it. Earlier when I didn't find him in the house I'd take it

for granted that he'd either gone out somewhere or
that he was up here on the terrace. You see sometimes he would stay on the terrace overnight and it
was bad for him.'

'Didn't you ask him not to?'

'I did—several times. But then I got used to it. And
gradually I also lost interest . . . Why are you surprised? It often happens—doesn't it?—the old ties remain but the interest goes out.' She held herself back,
suddenly scared she had gone too far. But after a moment of hesitation she resumed: 'The other day also I
presumed he was on the terrace, so I put the children
to sleep and went to bed. I wasn't much worried
when he didn't return the next day either. You see
he'd done it before—he'd go away for a couple of
days or so. Then on the third day I heard from the
hospital . . .'

She fell silent. The shadows had begun to darken
on our terrace but the church spires in the distance
still gleamed in the sun. The noises floating up from
the square below were subdued.

'Didn't you go to the hospital?'

'Yes—but it was too late by then. He was so far
gone he couldn't even recognize me.'

An uneasiness heaved within me.

'No parting word?'

She stared at me silently. 'None.'

'And the children . . .'

'I hadn't taken them along. I was afraid. Their presence would only have added to his suffering.' She
paused, threw me a glance and went on: 'He was always so worried about them. It was worse in his last
days.' When she looked up again her eyes reflected

my surprise. She was mildly amused. 'Why, don't you know we weren't married?' She laughed to see me stupefied. The laughter stopped, the silence went on: it washed away all the words and left them along banks humming with stillness.

Below us the square lights came on.

'You could do with a drink now!'

'Don't bother', I said uncertainly. 'I must get along in a short while.'

'Wait! I'll be back in a moment.'

She went downstairs. I sat alone, but not all alone, for I had her words for company. I recalled the far-off evening at the concert hall where I had met her husband. I remembered his silhouetted figure at the tram stand, his face turned towards me, and I remembered his eyes and the ironic smile on his lips. And suddenly it seemed he was standing right behind me on the terrace. I gave a start and turned round. But it was she, coming up the stairs. She had a bottle of whisky and two glasses with her.

'No soda in the house. You won't mind drinking it with water, do you?' she said, so matter-of-factly, yet warmly, as though we had known each other for years.

We drank in silence. It must have been the early tremulous darkness of summer-end or the glow of whisky which made us think we could come closer to each other, with him as a pretext—a palpable illusion, a make-believe—at least for the time being.

'Wasn't it this same time of the year when you met him?'

'Well, it was autumn then.'

'He'd often talk of you.'

'Oh! We hardly knew each other. We met only twice.'

'He knew so little about you he felt he could talk to you without reserve.'

It is possible that she was right. Men do choose some stranger to confide in. Perhaps I was his choice. A poor choice though, for I knew little of him till the end.

'But he didn't tell you much about himself, did he?'

'He talked of going back to Calcutta. But then everyone talks of going back to their country.'

She kept staring into the darkness, her glass in her hand. 'No, not that', she said finally, taking a small sip from her glass. 'He just couldn't make up his mind, you know. He didn't want to stay here but he didn't want to go back either.'

She took a long pull at her glass. Downstairs the noises of the children had subsided. I heard tram bells faintly in the distance.

'He was afraid', she said.

'Afraid of what?'

Her eyes returned to me. She put her glass down. 'Didn't he tell you he had a wife and an eight-year-old son in Calcutta? The boy would have been a year old when he came here for his training.'

'And you knew it all along?'

'Now, wouldn't I!' She laughed. 'There were letters. Sometimes he'd read them to me. My daughter has a snap of her half-brother. She even keeps it with her in bed.'

She poured us another drink. For the first time that evening I felt thirsty, my throat parched. The thirst came on blinking and swaying like an exhausted animal in a scalding expanse of desert.

'You wanted me to read you some letters.'

'Yes I had that in mind', she said apologetically. 'I can't read Bengali. I tried to learn it from him but left it off.'

'Whose letters are they?'

'I'll give them to you when we go downstairs. Sometimes they're from his wife, other times from his father. They know nothing yet.'

'Don't they know—'

'No, nothing of the sort. They must have waited every year for him to come back.'

It was now very dark on the terrace. Stars appeared in the sky as bright and clear as in the Indian sky above hill resorts.

'Have you ever been to Calcutta?'

'Yes, many years back. On a school trip.'

'Is it a very big city?' She looked at me with eager eyes.

'Yes it is—it's like any other big city.'

'He'd often tell the children about it—the Hugli river, the Howrah bridge, crowds on the bridge and so on'. She spoke in a monotone, roping in words in the lazy drawl which follows a few drinks. 'He told us rainwater runs so high on the roads that little children take dips in it—is that true?' Her eyes shone with a momentary excitement. 'What I don't quite get is why he wouldn't tell me what he told everybody else.' A quivering grievance swam across the corners of her eyes.

'What wouldn't he tell you?'

'About his wanting to go back. I wouldn't have come in his way. I'm happy as I am with my children.

He could have been happy there.'

Happy indeed! That night as we sat on the dark terrace the word sounded irrelevant; it did not belong;
the word had a sound but was empty of all meaning.
Her sari, the vermilion mark on her forehead, the
bangles—were those expressions of 'happiness', the
kind that waited for him somewhere in Calcutta?

I recalled what he had told me in the pub. 'He told
me once he owed his life to you.'

'Now that isn't true', she said, looking away. 'He
felt very close to me, that's all.'

She held up the bottle to pour me yet another
drink.

'No, I must leave now.'

'What! Leaving already?' She turned a pair of questioning eyes on me. 'You have to call on someone?'

'The children are all alone downstairs.'

'They must have dropped off to sleep . . . Come
on, it's almost finished. And anyway there's no one
else to drink it now.'

I tried to hold back her hand but as the whisky was
down almost to the bottom I saw no point in protest-
ing. So we upped and shared it.

'Did he drink?'

'I didn't know he did till after I came back from the
hospital and found this half-finished bottle stowed
away in his medicine cabinet.'

By now the square was deserted. I stepped over to
the parapet and put my glass on it. He was dead, but
the last of his whisky was in my glass. A man isn't
finished when he's dead; he dies a second time, and
for good, when other people finish for him what he
left unfinished.

I turned round. I could not see her. Her empty glass stood on the tripod. I ran my eyes all over the dark terrace but she was nowhere around. I began a long wait, not for her to come back but to find an opportune moment to leave.

I picked up both glasses, leaving the empty bottle behind. I searched the darkness again for anything that may have been left undone before I descended the stairs.

She was in the kitchen. The children had fallen asleep on the couch in the living room, the *tanpura* stood in the corner behind it, the hardbound notebook wrapped in red cloth lay on the table.

I could have read those letters for her but my courage drained away. Perhaps some other day, I told myself.

I did not go in to her. There really seemed nothing I could have gone to her for, nothing she could have come to me for.

Fear seized me as I left the house and I broke into a run. When I finally pulled myself together I had a good silent laugh at myself, standing still in the dark street. There was no one around, in front or behind. India was a long way ahead and he a long way behind.

I began walking on steady feet towards the tram stand.

*Translated by Kuldip Singh*

# Weekend

She raised the quilt off her face, lingering between sleep and wakefulness. The kisses of the receding night stuck like chunks between her teeth. She caressed them with the tip of her tongue, rolled them over in her mouth and bit, but no blood oozed out. All her blood had pooled round the rose between her thighs, the dark triangle wet with perspiration. She weaved her legs in between his, calling out to him softly. The intoxication of his touch, that which galloped like a stag within her, chased gilded illusions, endlessly, futilely.

She stretched out her arms, nestled his head on her breasts and opened her eyes. The dawn outside stretched like a grey cloud across the window. The three poplar trees which swayed in the breeze at night now stood still: leafless, dark silhouettes. These I'll remember, she told herself, these poplar trees, this pale morning. She held his face midway as it stole down her belly on its quest . . . And what else shall I remember? After the trees, this gallop of the deer inside me, the icecream cone, and a clean sunwashed slice of pain glittering in the grass. She took his earlobe between her lips and let his excitement trickle into her mouth.

When the alarm clock rang it startled them both, arresting the fluid motion of their bodies. It's nothing much when you are asleep, but when awake it sounds like an alarm, a warning, a little insistent animal screaming in the darkness of the room. Her hands upon him went numb. For a long moment after the clock gasped out its last note it didn't quite seem dead: it had stopped to recover its breath and would get going again. Finally she gathered enough courage to press down the alarm button. Only by then it wasn't necessary.

The clock had spent itself but she had not yet begun. She opened her eyes, touched the man by her side and took a cigarette from under the pillow, as though these preparatory actions would set her going. If you are in your own room and have slept in your own bed it isn't difficult to take up from where you left off at night. But in another person's room everything remains frozen, incomplete, something like a picture frame awaiting the picture or a first draft awaiting the precision of a cohesive meaning. The disorderly pile of her clothes, a glass half full of water, his naked arms—these with their burden of desire linked her with the night. She stared at them and thought: when he wakes up, he'll find me gone; I'll be at the far shore of the night and I'll call out to him, back here, to *this* shore where we are not strangers, where we know each other well.

Slowly she got out of bed. She stood before the mirror. Each morning revives anew the courage to go on. She put on her clothes, glanced at herself in the mirror and chose a lipstick to go with the hue that rose on the crest of the morning light. This she did always, in her room. But in his room his presence seemed to wind itself round her, layer on layer, and she came undone. 'This is our home', he would say, 'and you are mine.' There was no home anywhere; therefore his 'our' had a magical sound and the splendour of sunshine. 'You are mine', he said, and the sun reached out across the dense jungle where she stood, alone, in front of the mirror, choosing her lipstick.

Together they walked to the railway station. They spent their weekends in another city nearby. Once in the train they felt they had always been living together. He rested his head on her shoulder while she looked out. Close by lay the kit of toys, bread, biscuits and a sleeping-bag. Sometimes his mouth left its resting place at her shoulder and stole up her neck, obliterating consciousness of all but the fire of his lips.

These days they had to themselves. Out in the street people thought she was lonely and alone. She walked her way and no one could have guessed she was returning, not going away. Returning to her marginal life, dozing in the sun, and . . . And then she would stop in her tracks and think of the night they had shared together, another night that would come the next week, next Saturday, Sunday—as if these were the only words the wheels of the train beat out one after the other. Strange, isn't it, she thought, how the words rise, as they would when she was a child, from the wheels and then go down again, dying.

No one dies. Things return from the brink. Nor

does the day ever come to an end. The same hour returns the next day, panting, to sit at one's feet, like a pet dog broken loose from its chain who disappeared in the dark night. Like this day, captive in a railway compartment, with him, his eyelids drooping with sleep and the sun. Those half-closed eyes on which my lips would have closed if so many people hadn't been around. Can they know that this man with dozing head on my shoulder was on me last night, with an ocean stirring inside, surging forth, and he, a splinter of driftwood, rising on its waves, falling, dying?

No, no one dies. Not even the sign that comes up on the wind. It stays. It beckons to me and I go running to him.

'Wait here', he said. 'I'll just be back.'

She watched him go out of the park. They had been sitting there, by the stadium, since their train journey. 'I sit on a bench', she mused, 'and all around me is the grass, this pale green grass. And the row of electric poles, and far in the distance the boarding house. I sit as if this were my Sunday picnic. Some words carry a whole atmosphere with them. One such word is "picnic". It recalls to me the smell of burning leaves and laughter under the trees, the hum of descending darkness . . . This small miracle happened when we were on the train. I told him I wouldn't sit by myself on the bench this time, that he could bring his daughter out into the park and I'd watch them play together. She wouldn't have to know I came with her father. Only I'd know that. He needn't feel guilty about bringing another woman— not his own—when he visited his daughter.'

'You mean you won't mind it?'

'Why should I?', I said, laying my tired head on his shoulder.

Empty benches lay tier upon tier in the pavilion at the further end of the park, like those in a Roman amphitheatre. The red tin roof shone brightly in the sun. It was a day in March which sparkled the more as the sun rose.

She watched him go. Her heart went after him. 'I am', she repeated to herself like an incantation, 'I am here. He has come to see his daughter. They will play together till evening. I watch them play. We go back at night. I go at it again. He comforts me. He fills up the void within me even as it empties him.

'But this I didn't understand before. Then I'd importune him. Once I'd been with him in his room another five days my patience would have run out. How long shall we continue to see each other on the quiet, like thieves? Even thieves dare to come into the open sometimes. You must make up your mind one way or the other . . . And before long I'd be tearing at my clothes in a fit of exasperation, like thwarted children running round the room. Everything in the room appeared to come at me, gnashing its teeth. I gnashed my teeth at everything. He'd be scared. I'd see him scared and I'd begin to cry. I'd be scared to see him scared. I'd be scared I might lose him like his wife had. "No", I'd mumble, "you're all right as you are". He'd draw me into his arms. We'd hold fast, desperately, to each other. We'd explore each other in places where ghosts dwelt. They quavered under my lips and chattering teeth. I'd taste him afresh. Together we clambered up heights. When he'd near the peak I'd catch up with him. There we'd lie awhile at the top, cradled in each other's arms, alone the two of us, no ghosts any more, nor any rage, only the peace of silence. Afterwards, when we'd climbed down, I'd scrub myself with a towel where his desire wetted me. I scrubbed him also, his vulnerable body white like a child's, uninitiated, virginal-looking, in spite of a marriage behind him. It seemed incredible that other hands touched him before me, made love to him. Every crevice of my being haunted by *her* spectres is impaled on pain. I throw them all open. They come out.'

They came back. She saw them while they were still some distance away. Their voices rose on the breeze. Her heart sank. She got up from the bench. She sat down again. They were laughing. He was watching his daughter as she romped about, her ribbon blown high. A spot of blue, it approached her with the shifting circles of her run.

The girl suddenly froze, her breath held. The strained interval spun out to breaking point. She had seen her, a stranger, sitting on the bench, fixing her with an intent gaze. Her grip on her father's hand tightened. Her eyes lit up with more than the sun, shining with a startled light of their own.

Her gaze was still fastened on the girl. He stood behind his daughter. All around was the grass. At her back lay the emptiness of silence. It moved in closer and pressed on, confronting her as she sat on the bench. She made an effort to smile. The girl watched her struggle. Children terrified her. Particularly girls, for they might instinctively catch her out. In order that she could face up to her, look her straight in the eyes, she repeated to herself the familiar charm: she is his daughter, this man's whom I love, whom I love dearly, whom I . . . She stopped. The words suddenly stood divested of their magic, naked in their inadequacy. There was no comfort in sight.

He whispered something in the girl's ear. Perhaps he told her that the woman sitting on the bench was not a stranger, that she was known to him, and she should not be afraid. But the girl continued to stare at her, some deep thought knitting her brows. Her strained breathing eased somewhat, though. It struck her that even though the girl was so small, she had her own terms to go by. She stood up for them in all her aloneness. As alone as she was herself. Out on the battleground. Neither needed to offer any concession to the other.

The March breeze blew over the tree tops. Grass, which lay subdued under their shadows turned to sunshine. They left the woman alone. He was playing with his daughter. They were running among the dunes. At some distance slanted the red roof of the pavilion with the green-painted benches under it. And there were all those trees over which the breeze blew.

'Bored, are you?'

'He has left his daughter to come to me, as if suddenly reminded of my existence. I look up at him in surprise. I draw him from where he is within his world to my world of pain and he comes scrambling. The girl looks on, wide-eyed. "No", I say. I let go his hand. "No, I am not bored. I am all right. You go play with her. I am comfortable—really." '

She made herself comfortable, stretched out in the

sleeping-bag on the bench. Her hands were out to shell peanuts, and her eyes to see them both play, and to see his part of the pillow which was open to the breeze. The breeze filled it and it fluttered. The no-smell of the smell of his hair lingered on it. 'I reach out my hand. Slowly my fingers close round it . . . No, let go. Open your fist. It's an open day. You're so open-hearted. You can go anywhere you like in this wide open world.

'How easy! I shove away *that* part of the sleeping-bag. I see them. They are outside me. He buys ice-cream, one cone for the girl, another for me. For a moment the distance between us disappears. We've stepped across it! We could be friends! Icecream smudges her mouth. He laughs happily at her. I wipe her mouth. She looks up at me. A strange fear still peeps out of her eyes. She wants to be friends with me but can't get over her fear. Coward! I suppress my anger and pull the thorn of fear out of her. Then I see. I see her soul splashed with red blood. And just as quickly I put the thorn back. She goes back into herself. I go back to my place. Alone, once again. Shivering, despite the March sun. I pull the sleeping-bag round me.

'How easy! I can go anywhere. Every path is open to me. I have no encumbrances, unlike him—a sepa-rated wife, a child with attachments and me in between. Filling the emptiness. Like the air which re-sides even in desolate corners of the earth. And when the world lays claim to the space it doesn't complain. It leaves, goes somewhere else.

'But I'll not go anywhere. My place is here, in this corner of the park, under the bright open sky, their

voices rippling over the breeze to me. This is my
weekend, of which no one can deprive me. I've learnt
to receive that man in me, like little children learn
walking. But this is no learning. Suddenly one day
the knees are up in the air. His presence crowds out
the five-day-of-the-week vacuity. Empty himself, he
fills me and in the process is himself filled. What
would it have been like had we lived together under
the same roof. Then perhaps there wouldn't have
been the fear of falling, hurting my knees, the awareness of a sprawling emptiness within. And then
would I have learnt either? I'm not so sure. Now even
as I stand still I feel I'm walking alongside him. And
when I do walk by his side I find I've hardly moved.'

But they had. They had gone over to the merry-go-
round. Their voices did not carry now, only some
shouts rose above the rustling of the leaves. They sat
astride the horses, those red and blue painted horses
of wood, along with the motor cars and aeroplanes,
swerving out and in in an uneven arc. They looked like
puppets from there, chasing each other, borne up in the
air.

'Now he stands quite close to the edge. He gives her
horse a slight push. It moves away from him. But not
far enough towards insecurity. No, there is no fear in
the girl's squeals. They always stop short at the edge
of fear, light as wings gliding through the air, bright
as day. They are a pretence of fear, not fear itself.'

Unawares, jealousy began to smoulder in her,
something she thought she had outgrown. She pulled
the sleeping-bag close over her so as to smother it.

It was dark inside. An isle of darkness, clean, warm
with her breath, intimate. 'Something is wrong

somewhere', she thought. 'So utterly wrong that it
looks almost like being the right thing.'

She rummaged in the dark and took out her happiness. She held it thoughtfully on her palm as if it were
a base coin. She flipped it up, listening intently the
while, her ear close to it, to make out if it produced
the right kind of clink. She strained her ear as though
everything depended on the sound it would catch.
But there was only the hum of the late noon silence.
And the girl's merry squeals, far lighter than wings.
Those squeals rang genuine. Her own darkness was
spurious.

'Sleeping—are you?' He shook her, laughing. She
woke. The shadows had lengthened. The breeze had
died down over the tree tops. The leaves drooped.
The benches, vacant earlier, now looked definitely
deserted.

'Let's go.'

They looked at each other, a full day gone from
them. The girl stood apart, withdrawn, behind her
father. The biscuit, cake and fruit boxes, with red rib-
bons knotted round them, which they had bought
yesterday, were now in the girl's hands. Their contents would last her a week. 'From one day of the
week to its next. An orderly succession of days. I
keep a count of them. Perhaps she does too.'

She looked at the girl more intently. She saw her as
if for the first time. The girl looked fragile, rather
pale, lips parted like the lid of a tiny box forced out to
a chink. But her eyes were large with black irises. In
profile she looked somewhat dishevelled, like her
father: regularity of line was not a strong feature with
either. The hair at the back of her head stuck out in a
duck's tail.

She touched her hair for the very first time. The girl moved in a feeble attempt to shake off her hand but then, soon, stopped. She realized the time had come to leave and resistance futile. Children smell their lot much as dogs their death, and both stop struggling after a certain point.

They left. Hands waved briefly in the air. The girl's diffident, sorrowful. Sorrow grated like sand. The sunwashed sand. It smeared his face. He held her by the finger. He turned around.

'He looks at me inquiringly. "You'll wait there for me, won't you?" he asks in a whisper. "I'll leave her at the boarding-house and be back in no time".'

His voice is too low for the girl to make out anything. But a certain suspicion wells up in her eyes as she watches her father. In that moment, the briefest, she looked upon him, her own father, as a stranger—like the rest of the world . . .

'It's all right, though. Sooner or later she'll have to face it. Some day when she's grown up and looks at herself in a mirror she'll find this noon peep out of it at her and remember how when she was a small child a certain woman, a complete stranger to her, came with her father once and stayed lying down on the grass the whole day; that woman never came again, but on that one occasion we ate icecream together. How surprising, that small things loom large in one's memory even after one has grown up. Like a certain sunshine, some peanut shells, the fluttering corner of a certain sleeping-bag, a certain icecream cone.'

Someone was shouting in the courtyard behind the bar. In the square opposite the voices, which had come muffled to her in the park, were pitched harsh like fragments of glass, catching the last of the sun. She would wait for him. He had asked her to wait for him in this bar of an alien city. The place stank with stale beer. People at the other tables stole glances at her now and then. A young woman, alone, at the window, looking out.

She waited. She ordered beer to keep away the awareness of those glances. Far out in the distance was the boarding-house. Tall glass windows. A long, high perimeter topped with broken glass. That girl lives behind the high wall. She sipped at her beer.

Presently she saw his shadow draw near across the square.

She gazed fixedly at the man crossing the square. The flagstones awash in the haze of the departing sun. A man walking across the gleaming stones. A woman sipping her beer, looking out at the man . . . And then it filled her with the wonder of a miracle that this man was *hers*, that he was coming to *her*. So wonderful she could hardly believe it! It looked like a frozen scene from some movie. As the celluloid runs out its spool a certain picture occupies the screen. Forever the same. A woman looking out of the window, a man walking across the square, the flagstones touched with the brilliance of the departing sun, his shadow across the stones—all these are imperishable. 'No one can take these away from me. Neither that girl nor his wife. These are my stones: none but I can decipher the hieroglyph on them.

'I felt his breath over me. Eyes closed, I could tell him by his breath, as indeed by the smell of his clothes. The first thing I noticed was the agitated look on his face as he came in. At once he downed two mugs of beer one after the other. Then he touched me on the spot of my shoulder where his lips pressed when he made love to me, and a feeble smile appeared on his lips. "Was I gone too long?" His eyes rested on me. His voice had a faint quiver in it. "I wanted her to go to sleep before I left". My eyes enveloped him and his pain. "Did she go to sleep?" I asked. He hesitated. He was a bad liar. I remember the first time I asked him if he was married. His hesitation was so ludicrous I almost laughed, for I didn't care a hang about his marriage so long as he was with me. But I was eager to see his daughter. I am an eager sort of person. I like the sound of that word. Sometimes, though, I think that those who are eager seldom meet a happy end.

'What end is happy? He was still looking at me. I made up my mind I wouldn't stop him from drinking. I'd let him drink his fill. Occasionally we drank in his room, thirsty after we'd made love. He'd come to sit on the edge of the bed. I'd touch his naked back with my lips. Soon they'd be roaming all over, one shoulder blade to the other. His body, so white and vulnerable, looked virginal despite his marriage— perhaps I've already said this. I'd kiss the flesh over his heart. It rippled like a small fish. And it dinned with the blood rushing about in it. I could hear it inside him when he'd be inside me.'

'Had she gone to sleep?' I asked again. A splinter of the retreating sun wedged itself in through the window. It lay on his palm. He shook it away. 'No'. He shook his head. 'She . . . she started crying when I was about to leave. She hid her face behind my fingers. I stood there while she sobbed. Can you hear her? I stood outside on the landing. I waited for her to quieten down, until the warden asked me to leave, for the longer I hung about the more hopeful she'd become that I'd stay back with her. I started going down the stairs. . . '

'What wilderness it must be', I thought, 'where she lives, alone—where even the faintest rustling of the leaves must be like a portent of disaster.' My bare hand retreated from his face to the table. We'd lost contact. He'd retreated into himself, closing the door behind him and bolting it from the inside. I stood outside, my ear to the door. 'As I went down the stairs . . .', he was saying from behind it.

'I can hear. But when we'd be together in bed at night, those sobs which descended the stairs with him would stop short and turn on their heels. I believe in my body more than I do in anything else. It will bring him back to me, spellbound.

'But not now. This moment there's no contact between us. Our hands lie idle. Besides, there are so many people around in the restaurant. I am like dust in their presence. A mere speck, knocking at a closed door, or hovering over the sobs descending the stairs.'

She counted the stairs as she climbed up. She had done it many times before—when going up at night or down in the morning. His small room lay between a narrow passage leading up to it and a terrace. There was a basin on one side of the passage and over it a looking-glass nailed to the wall. Close to the faucet his shaving tools ('How he laughed at my use of the word!') were scattered on the basin. He put out his socks and underwear to dry on the terrace. Beyond it stood the three poplar trees, their branches intertwined.

'I climb the stairs. The lamp-post has been lit. A dappled shadow is cast across the bed and half-way up the wall. It sways as the breeze rises. He is asleep beside me. I bend over his face and set out on my solitary journey across the desert between his sleep and my waking . . .

'How different were those days in the beginning! It was early summer when we first met. When winter came along I thought it was time we made a final decision. Either he'd have to be with me where I am, on this side of the night, or choose to remain on the other where we meet stealthily after dark, the other side with bleak weekends, a weeping girl, a shuttle train.

'Then the trees shed their old leaves and put on new ones. While we made love to each other the seasons shrank into the distance like trees by the roadside. So too the sobs which had lingered on the stairs.

'There was a time, though, when I resolved not to see him any more, not even to raise my eyes to his face or turn round if we ever ran into each other in the street—as if he were thin air I could walk on through, eyes closed . . . But when I opened my eyes, he was where he had been, with me heavy inside him like a brooding silence. He turned on his side, blinking at me. "Want to go?" he said sleepily.—"No! We still have some hours of the night left to us. Listen", I continued after a pause, "are you still thinking about it?"—"About what?" he asked, mildly surprised.— "When you were going down the stairs", I mumbled, "those sobs followed you. The girl was crying".

'He said nothing. I went out and walked headlong on. I came to a halt. It was dark all around but for a yellow wick flame flickering in the middle of the passage. Below it in the corner was the telephone, cold, impersonal and frightening—like the black future— drawing me towards it.

'I picked up the receiver. The operator's voice came through. "Number, please. Which city?" The air crackled between us. It spanned the distance between the two cities and froze as the numbers clicked and another voice asked, "Who is it?"

'I brushed the question aside with a sweep of my hand. "Look", I said, "all I want to know is whether she has gone to sleep, or is she still crying?"

"Which girl are you talking about? There are one hundred and fifty children here".

'One hundred and fifty children! Hurriedly I put the receiver back in its cradle. One hundred and fifty children stretched out in a dormitory from one end to the other! I followed them, up in the dark aisle, in search of that one name which had a face, a girl's, who had played in the sun earlier in the day with her father. Then I burst out laughing. In that darkness, laughing all by myself, I discovered that pain alone is what neither diminishes nor increases when shared— it only comes out more clear and sparkling clean.

'I turned round, suddenly light and carefree. Back in the room I sat by him in the bed, wrapped in my blanket. A grubby morning began to fill the window. I watched the poplar trees emerge out of darkness. Sometimes a person feels closer to death than to life.

He does not die, but his whole life whirls past him like a merry-go-round, with its lost opportunities and the distances he could not span pursuing one another like the wooden horses with the same distances in between as in the beginning: none can catch up with the other and take hold of it.

'I take hold of him. He draws me into the warmth of his arms. "Are you leaving already?" His voice still smells of yesterday's sunshine, of the grass, of the time spent together. "I'll come again", I reassure him. I am happy I can leave him before his smell can get stale. I'll come back next week but right now I can go—to my lonely room and the cold, unslept-in bed. I am really surprised at the couples who have to put up with each other day after day. They have no interludes in which to recoup their sense of wonder at the other's body. True, this continuity makes for a family. But I suppose I'm not cut out for the intimacy of a warm, conjugal bed. No, that's not for me.

'For me there are weekends, like so many incandescent lamp-posts spaced out in the darkness. They are put out as the day breaks. So must I gather my sleeping-bag, the purse and the toothbursh and leave. I leave early in the morning like a thief so that the neighbours may not see me come out of his apartment.

'I look about the room for one last time before leaving. My eyes rove over his face turned towards the wall, my half of the pillow dimpled, some old toys the girl needs no longer, a few books I leave behind me every week, and the three poplar trees once green with leaves but now bare. Spring will return, and find me waiting for the summer. Autumn will be back too, followed by the short misty days of winter.'

She descended the stairs and came out into the street. The clamour of the street gave her a strange comfort. Men going out to work, the clanging trams, children going out to school. Occasionally someone looked at her, wondering perhaps at where a lonesome young woman should be going so early in the morning.

'No, I am not going away. I am coming back.'

*Translated by Kuldip Singh*

# An Inch And a Half Above Ground

'Please do sit down. There's room enough for the two of us. After all how much room does a man need? No you won't be in my way. Not at all; and you don't have to talk to me unless you want to. I'm fond of silence myself. In fact we could talk and keep quiet simultaneously. Of course very few people know how to do that. But I've been doing just that for years. No I don't expect . . . you . . . you are young. At your age silence *means* silence.

'I notice you have a small mug of beer before you. I guess you've not caught the disease yet. I can see you're a stranger to this place. I recognize all the habitues, specially those that come in at this late hour. One can't talk to them. They're too far gone before they arrive. They come in for their last drink because all the other pubs are closed. Many of them pass out very soon. I've often helped carry some of them out.

'Please don't misunderstand me. I wasn't insinuating anything. You seem to have come here for the first time and I saw you sitting all by yourself. That's why I asked you to come over and join me. You needn't fear me imposing on you. We could remain alone with our drinks even while sitting at the same table. I concede that's a bit difficult at my age, for old men are in constant fear. Growing gradually old with dignity isn't given to everybody. It's an art that needs acquiring.

'I beg your pardon? My age? Let's have your guess. Oh, no; Of course I feel flattered.

'I think I'll have another drink. What about you? You won't? Well I can't press you. I believe every man should be free to choose his own life and his own drink, and both choices can be made only once. After that we just keep repeating them.

'Do you believe in life after death? I hope you won't give me the usual answer about not holding to any religion. I'm a Catholic myself but I'm fascinated by your faith in not really dying after being dead . . . that one has in fact many lives. At night I think of this question often.

'You can imagine that at my age one doesn't sleep well. For that one needs a measure of carefreeness and half a measure of fatigue. In the absence of these one tries to make do with a measure and a half of beer. That's why I come here every midnight . . . have been doing so for the last fifteen years. Of course I *do* get some sleep, but at about three in the morning I invariably wake up. That's a terrible hour. Two means there's still night ahead; four means you start expecting the morning; but at three you're neither here nor there. I've always thought that the hour of death.

'I beg your pardon? No I don't live alone. I have a cat—have had it for years now. Just think . . . while I sit here talking of this and that she must be waiting for me at the doorstep.

'Isn't that funny? I can't say what you think but it's quite a consolation to me that someone's waiting for

me back home. I can't conceive of a person who
doesn't wait for someone or for whom someone
doesn't wait. Waiting or being awaited is what life's
all about.

'Now, these cats wait for long and with patience.
Just like women. There's a great similarity in other
respects too; both can greatly attract and frighten us.

'Of course you fear dogs and other animals too.
But that's an inferior kind of fear. You shun the dog
and the dog shuns you; there's a mutual distrust. But
there's hardly any mystery or thrill in that fear of the
kind you have on seeing a cat or snake.

'To tell you the truth—and I *am* speaking from
experience—you can't know a woman or a cat even
after a lifetime of companionship. Not because they
wilfully hide things from you but because you yourself lack the courage to open the door which leads to
their inmost mystery.

'Well I hope you won't mind my having another
drink. They'll close very soon and not a drop will be
going in the city until morning. Please have no fear. I
know my limit. You see one should be able to rise
above the ground, just about an inch and a half. Not
more than that, else one might soar to the heights of a
police station, which wouldn't be too pleasant.

'But there *are* people who keep their feet planted
out of fear. Drink's wasted on them. The right distance is an inch and a half. One must always be conscious enough to see one's consciousness going off,
like a matchstick, which needs dropping when the
flame reaches the fingers. The secret of good drinking
lies in your ability to stop at the right time. The problem is we don't know the right time till we're an inch

and a half above. Knowledge comes with loss of knowledge, or something like that.

'You can laugh it away if you like. I've learnt the only way of feeling secure is to be ignorant of certain things. But one learns that gradually, even as one learns to live with one's wife in the same house for years despite a lurking suspicion that she's playing your game too.

'Sometimes you fall in love with a second or a third woman to be rid of that suspicion. But it's like a game of chess. You play a hand and your adversary has an infinity of choices. Well not exactly an infinity but . . . choices all the same. You lose a game and hope you won't lose the next. You forget every game has its own possibilities, numerous and mysterious as those of every other. which is why I believe that no matter how many women you fall in love with you really fall in love with the same woman again and again.

'I beg your pardon? Well no. As I said I live all by myself, excepting of course my cat. Yes. I'm married but my wife is dead—or at least that's my conjecture.

'You look a bit mystified. It's conjecture because I didn't see her die. As long as you don't see her die or bury her yourself you only guess she's dead. You may laugh but it seems to me that short of watching her die and burying her with your own hands you're eternally doomed to the hope that she's still alive. That you'll enter the house some day and she'll be there, running out of the kitchen to meet you, wiping her hands on an apron!

'I've heard people say that time heals almost everything. Perhaps it does. But I think it doesn't heal as much as sweep things away into dark corners or under the carpet. That its claws are always ready to pounce upon you all of a sudden, any moment.

'It may be that I'm just talking nonsense. That's thanks to beer. You go astray and then keep going round and round the same spot: You know the game in which children sit in a circle and one of them goes round and round with a handkerchief or something? You have this game in your country too? Now isn't that something? No matter what be the distance children's games are the same!

'Well in those days all of us seemed involved in this game. Nobody was sure when they'd leave their trap and behind whom, on the sly. Each one kept looking at his back, like children in that game, for the hidden trap.

'Yes I'm talking of the time when the Germans came to this country. You must've been young then. Not that I was very old at the time. And I used to be strong as a bull and busy through the day with my work. There's an age when everybody feels satisfied with commonplace happiness, when one doesn't have time to look beyond that. Until the time comes when that commonplace pleasure isn't possible.

'You must've noticed happiness is a matter of particular moments. It seems solid while those moments last but gets tasteless and dim like a hangover with those moments behind you. But pain and suffering are independent of particular moments. I mean at the time they come you don't really feel it. I mean when they come you're just stunned, you can't fit them into patterns or frameworks.

'You needn't rush to conclusions. I'm not suggesting I saw my wife undergo torture. In fact when I got home that day they'd already taken her away. That was the first time in seven years of our marriage that I'd come into the house and she wasn't there.

'The neighbours . . . I could see them peering out of their windows at me. That was natural. I was equally curious about people whose relatives were whisked away by the Gestapo in a closed van. But I hadn't imagined I'd return home to find my wife's room empty some day.

'I beg your pardon? Well, I knew you'd ask me that. In fact if you hadn't, I'd have been surprised. No sir, I didn't quite grasp the situation at first. Didn't I tell you that when a calamity comes one is only stunned to begin with. Stunned and witless, so to speak. I could see all her things scattered around. Her clothes, her books, old newspapers. The closets were all open, all sorts of things rifled out of them and lying about on the floor. Christmas gifts, sewing machine, an old album. Well you know one accumulates all sorts of things after one's married. It was clear they'd conducted a very thorough search.

'That night I sat in my room. Her bed was unmade. Under her pillow I found her matchbox and a packet of cigarettes. She smoked just before sleeping. At first I was irritated by this habit but soon I'd got used to it. On a table near the bed was the book she was reading. She'd used a hairpin as a bookmark. The smell of her hair clung to that hairpin.

'You know how one recollects little, insignificant details after years. That's as it should be. Before you're married you think only of big and important things; after a companionship over the years all those big things slip out and you're left with trivial habits, seemingly unimportant routines, little mutual secrets you can't share with anyone else but without which you feel absolutely desolate.

'That night I spent alone, surrounded by her things, lost to what had happened. She wasn't there. That I could see. But I couldn't grasp the fact that they'd actually taken her away. After all why *my* wife? I kept repeating the stupid question to myself all night.

'Later I learnt the Gestapo had discovered banned pamphlets and papers which used to be distributed among people in secret. And I'd never known about those things! We'd slept in the same bed and made love there, and I didn't know her secrets. Didn't know she had any I didn't share? Doesn't it strike you as funny that they knew my wife better than I did?

'Let me finish my glass and I'll keep you company. It's going to be closing time soon. No we needn't hurry. One should always enjoy one's drink. We have a saying in our language: Drink heartily for in a hundred years you won't be here.

'A hundred years! Quite some time, you'll admit. I doubt either of us will live that long. A man lives, eats, drinks and then the time comes when he's done for. No sir it's not death that's terrible. What's terrible is that the people who die take their secrets with them and we can't do anything to them. Hundreds of people die every day without your being any the worse for it.

'That night I kept walking from one room to the other in my house. You'll laugh when I tell you that I too gave her belongings a thorough search.

'Imagine, I was searching her room just like another secret service man! I couldn't accept the fact that I'd never be able to ask her anything. What terrified me that day was not the certainty of her death but the uncertainty of my knowledge of her. Death will seal her off for ever against my probing.

'Next day they came again. I was waiting for them. Had she confessed everything they wouldn't have needed me. But I knew she wouldn't open her mouth. I might have been ignorant of her secret but I knew her habits. She knew how to keep her mouth shut in the face of every horrible torture.

'The first question they asked me was quite straight. Was I so-and-so's husband? Yes I was. The others I knew nothing about.

'But they wouldn't let me off so easily. They mocked my ignorance of her secret activities. They were sure I was pretending ignorance to save my skin.

'They took me to a solitary cell. And for a week, day and night, they pestered me with the same question in different ways: What did I know about her movements? Who were her colleagues? Who had passed those papers to her?

'But I won't tell you the methods they used to extract an answer. I won't because details wouldn't help you understand. You couldn't understand.

'Well they beat me till I was unconscious and then they waited patiently till I was conscious again and then they beat me again, and so on. They couldn't believe I knew nothing.

'No I'm not complaining about the pain. My pain was that I had nothing to keep back from them. I could only tell them a few very ordinary things which every husband knows about his wife and shares with her. If they hadn't arrested her I would have continued to think she was what I thought she was.

'Those were the last days of the war you know, and the Gestapo didn't easily release anybody or kill anybody without finding out everything. My wife it seems didn't open her mouth at all. They despaired of her but had hopes of breaking me. They didn't seem keen about finishing me off but short of that they gave me all they had. I didn't confess anything. I didn't have anything to confess. The realization that she'd kept me in the dark kept hurting.

'Earlier, the realization that she'd kept me in the dark had hurt. But later, in the midst of the torture I was grateful she hadn't told me anything.

'I still can't decide whether I had the guts to stay quiet if she'd told me her secret. Imagine my agony if the choice to confess had existed! One can bear suffering when there is no way out. But suppose you know you can put an end to your suffering by betraying your wife or your father or your brother or your lover? Suppose you know that? It's hard to say you won't take that way out. Did she keep me in the dark to spare me the agony of that choice?

'You don't think so? Well, it's possible I'm wrong. But you see at night, when I can't sleep, that thought consoles. Ah well, you can't understand this. When I asked you to join me I had no hope I'd make you understand what I feel.

'I beg your pardon? Well no, I never saw her again. One noon on my way home I happened to see that poster. They used to paste those posters every third or fourth day. They carried a list of about thirty or forty people who'd been shot dead the night before. When I saw my wife's name on that poster it struck me as odd that behind a simple name lay my wife. As I said, unless you see someone die before your eyes you aren't convinced . . . a vague hope persists that when you enter a room . . .

'But let me not repeat myself. Thanks to beer you keep going round and round the same point, round and round and round.

'You aren't leaving? Well let me buy a few pieces of salami for my cat.

'No you needn't see me home. It's not too far from here. I know my limit. Didn't I tell you—just enough to lift you an inch and a half above ground.'

*Translated by Krishna Baldev Vaid*

# The Difference

On getting off the bus he found himself standing in front of the Town Hall. A long, monstrous building. On its first floor a row of windows with dingy glass panes reflecting the evening sun that looked even dingier. A few yards away from where he stood a pub, a barber's shop and two general stores.

'When is the last bus for Prague?' he asked the conductor of the bus that had brought him there.

'At ten.'

He started walking towards the shops. This was his first visit to the place, but everything looked very familiar. All small towns look alike, he thought. The town hall, the church, the square, and a vacant drowsiness.

The wind was cold although it was late May. He took out his muffler from the duffel bag. He did not want to put on his gloves yet. If he missed the last bus he would sleep somewhere in the open in his sleeping bag. Far better than going to a hotel, he thought. Unless, of course, it was too cold.

Last summer, during their trip together to Moravia, they had always slept out in the open. In the same sleeping bag. She had got used to it. They had spent all their savings from hotels on beer.

Last summer, yes.

He wrapped the muffler carefully round his neck and ears. It's quite chilly, he thought. But not unbearable, not even for her. First she was quite scared. Now she must be all right. No fears now. No fears, he repeated to himself.

He lingered awhile outside a grocer's, scanning the show-window. Then he thought of something and walked in. Of course he had not expected fresh fruit. Not in that season. He picked up a tin each of peaches and pineapple. And half a kilo of salami. And a few slices of French cheese, her favourite cheese. How she used to nibble at it constantly, everytime she stayed overnight in his room.

Just as he was leaving the store he remembered something. A packet of Lipa. She would be out of cigarettes in the hospital.

He was feeling a bit thirsty now. There's enough time, he thought, at least enough for a small beer. He walked across the square to the pub.

'A small beer, please.'

The barman picked up a mug and put it under the tap. When the beer began to froth over the brim he turned off the tap, wiped the mug with a rag and thumped it before him on the counter.

The beer was rather stale and tepid, but not too bad after all. The barman was now biting on a sausage. Middle aged. Tearful, blue eyes.

'How do I get to the hospital, please?'

The barman gave him a hard look. Then his eyes became fixed on the sleeping-bag.

'You' are from Prague, eh?'

He nodded.

The barman's look was suspicious.

'On the right side of the Town Hall, a little further away from the cometery', he said at last.

'Is it very far?'

The barman raised his half-bitten sausage in a vulgar gesture and said, 'Just one kilometre.' Then he began to laugh.

Outside he noticed the brightness of spring. Brightness without that strain you have in summer. A light, fresh glow that comes only after a long winter.

He was not so nervous now, as he had been in the bus. The beer had cheered him up, he thought.

On reaching the cemetery he lit a cigarette. Then he shifted the bag from one shoulder to the other. He looked at the trees in the cemetery, their leaves dappled with the fading sunshine. On the road there were a few puddles left by the thaw. And the ruts of lorries and trucks. He rolled up his trousers and thought how surprised she would be to see him; perhaps pleased too. Perhaps. He could not be sure. Before leaving Prague she had forbidden him to come. She did not want to arouse any suspicions, she had said. They had decided she would spend a couple of days in the hospital and then return to Prague, and nobody would know where she had been.

He stopped before the hospital gate. Situated on a hillock, the building looked more like a college hostel, intimate and flawless, without the chilly bareness of hospitals.

He unrolled his trousers and entered. He noticed the flowerpots in the lobby and the slanting shadows of the columns. He walked up to the reception desk with great hesitation. The receptionist, a woman in a nurse's uniform, was absorbed in a newspaper. She looked at him from across her paper.

'Whom do you want to see?'

He mentioned the name. He felt she was not just a nurse but a woman in the uniform of a nurse. The thought was reassuring.

She had taken out a list.

'Is she in the maternity ward?'

He remained indecisively silent for a while and wiped his forehead.

'I don't know. This is my first visit. Can you find out from the list?'

Of course  he need not have said that. She was already scanning the list.

'Your wife's name is not on the maternity ward list'. The nurse gave him a questioning look.

'She is not my wife . . .', he said. 'I mean we are not married yet.'

He smiled in despair. Then he realized that his clarification was irrelevant as well as stupid.

The nurse gave him a curt glance and pushed back her hair.

'You should have said so to begin with', she observed in a tone that was not irritated but coldly aloof. She took out another list and asked him to repeat the name.

He stood waiting in silence.

'First floor, on your right, in the surgical ward', she said with a casual glance at him, and turned to her newspaper.

He began mounting the stairs.

There were open doors on both sides. Women sat

on their beds. In front of the doors hung washed nylon stockings, brassieres, underwear. The atmosphere was heavy with a sour, slimy odour of the kind that comes from the bodies or clothes of women working in the house. Red buckets filled with sand hung from the iron railing. Must be for fire, he thought.

Just as he reached the surgical ward someone from behind held him by the hand. He turned round with a start. It was a doctor.

'Whom do you want to see?' he asked.

He repeated the name.

'I see', said the doctor. 'But you'll have to leave this outside'. He pointed to his sleeping-bag.

He unloaded his back and placed the sleeping-bag in a corner.

'What do you have in that?'

He quietly pushed the duffel bag towards the doctor.

The doctor glanced at the contents and laughed a little.

'So . . . you are the man', he switched from his own language to English.

'I'm afraid I don't understand . . .'

'It's all right', he said in his own language. 'Bed 17. You've just thirty minutes; she's still very weak. You may go in now. His tone was very businesslike.

But he could not bring himself to enter the ward immediately. For a few moments he stood there, holding the bag in his hands like a child.

There was an empty chair near the door opening on a hall divided into cubicles by pink curtains. The cubi-

cles were lit by dim lights. He saw a stretcher in a
corner. A few dirty bandages lay on the stretcher.
Some nurse must have forgotten to pick them up, he
thought.

He entered the ward. With the sleeping-bag off his
back he felt very light. He lingered a moment in front
of Bed 17. There was no stir from it. She must be
asleep he thought.

For a second he could not see her.

He was standing beside a huge bed, smooth and
white and flat. He could not decide where the pillow
was. He had a fleeting thought that the bed was empty.

But it was not. Her head emerged from the sheets,
then her eyes. She was looking at him. Then a brief
smile appeared on her lips. She had recognized him.

She pointed to the stool with her eyes. He saw a
cup of milk there.

'Won't you drink that?' he said.

'Later. Put it down.'

He sat down on the stool, close beside her.

'When did you reach here?'

'Just a while ago . . .'

He looked at her dry lips.

'When was it?' he asked.

'In the morning . . . Take off your coat.'

He took off his coat and placed it on the bag behind
the stool. The window was closed. He caught sight
of her suitcase, the one she had brought with her
from Prague.

'It didn't take too long, did it?' he asked.

'No . . . they gave me chloroform. I didn't feel
anything.' she said.

'Didn't I tell you wouldn't feel anything? But you had your fears.' He tried to smile.

She kept looking at him, steadily.

'I had forbidden you to come', she said.

He bent forward and kissed her blonde hair, then her lips. Her face was very cold. He kissed her several times. She lay quietly with her head on the pillow.

'Are you happy now?' Her voice was very feeble.

'We were happy even before this', he said.

'Yes . . . but are you happy now?'

'Well, you know . . . it was the best way for both of us . . . I said so even then.'


The sheet slid off her breasts. She was wearing a green night-dress with black embroidered flowers. Those flowers once awoke a sweet tension in his body in his room. He was kissing her eyes now.

'Would you like a slice of cheese?'

'No . . . later'. She looked at the things on her bed.

'You shouldn't neglect your diet for a few days', he said.

'Nobody asked after me there, I hope?'

'No . . . no one knows you're here', he said.

She looked at him. Then she pulled his hand under the sheet and placed it softly on her stomach.

'Do you notice any difference?' she asked. His hand was lying on her bare, soft stomach.

'Was it painful?'

'No'. And she laughed feebly. 'I feel very light now. There's nothing inside here.'

He looked at her, at the dry lipstick on her lips. He withdrew his hand from under the sheet, quietly.

'You shouldn't strain yourself talking', he said.

'I feel so light now', she said.

'Did the doctor say anything?' he asked.

'No . . . except that if I'd come a month sooner it wouldn't have made me so weak.'

'Do you feel very weak?' he asked.

'No, I just feel very light now.'

'I'd told you to come over earlier but you kept postponing it', he said.

'You're always right', she answered.

He looked away from her in silence.

'You're offended?' She supported herself on her elbows.

'No . . . but you shouldn't strain yourself by talking', he said, caressing her hair.

'Listen . . . now there's nothing to worry about', she said. 'I'm all right now.'

'But you keep thinking about it', he said.

'I don't keep thinking about anything', she said. Then she unbuttoned his coat. 'You aren't wearing a sweater?'

'It wasn't too cold today.' he said.

They were silent for some time. A nurse came in. A cheerful looking blonde. After a look at both of them she approached the bed.

'You shouldn't sit up like this yet', she said, and put the raised head back on the pillow. Then she looked at him. 'Too much strain might be harmful.'

'I'll be leaving very soon', he said.

The nurse looked at the things lying on the bed. She turned to him and smiled. 'You should be more careful in future', she said.

He did not say anything and avoided her eyes.

Just before leaving the nurse paused. 'You have enough cotton?'

'Yes sister, thanks.'

The nurse left the cubicle.

'Just turn away for a second', she said. She was taking something from under the pillow.

'Shall I wait outside?' he asked.

'No, just turn your head a little', she said.

He turned his head to the wall. He was reminded of those nights, long ago, when she would get up from his bed and he would listen to the rustle of her clothes with his face averted.

'It's all right now', she said.

He pulled the stool closer to her pillow. He noticed a strange odour. Then he saw the pot under her bed. It was full of blood-soaked cotton. He couldn't believe it was all her blood.

'Do you still . . . ?' He did not complete the sentence.

'No . . . now it's much less.'

He bent down and pushed the pot further beneath the bed.

'Have you a cigarette?' she asked.

He took out two from the packet, lit them together and gave one to her.

'Are you allowed to smoke here?'

'No . . . but they don't bother me.' she had a long, deep puff. Her nostrils trembled as she exhaled the smoke. She asked him to throw the cigarette into the pot.

'I can't smoke.' A thin, feeble smile fluttered on her lips.

He extinguished the cigarette before throwing it

away. There was a faint touch of her lipstick on its tip.

'Have a slice of cheese.'

'No . . . you must leave now.'

'I will soon. There's still time.'

She had closed her eyes. The long brown lashes on that pale face reminded him of the eyelashes of a wax doll.

'Are you sleepy?' he asked softly.

'No . . . ' she opened her eyes. Putting her hand in his she started to rub it slowly.

'I knew you'd come', she said.

He kept looking at her.

'Listen . . . now we shall be able to live as before.' There was a hint of surprise in her tone.

'You remember', he said with a slight pressure on her hand, 'we wanted to go to Italy last summer. We can do that now.'

'Now we can go anywhere', she looked at him. 'Now there's no obstacle at all.'

Her tone struck him again as a little odd. But she was smiling, and that reassured him.

He heard the creaking of the wheelchair in the corridor outside. Someone in the neighbouring cubicle was screaming. A woman entered their cubicle, but seeing him went hurriedly out.

He looked at his watch and picked up his overcoat.

'You must eat the fruit and cheese', he said in English.

She nodded.

'Did you understand what I said?'

'You said You must eat the fruit and cheese.' She repeated his sentence in English. They laughed.

He wrapped the muffler round his neck, picked up the empty bag, hung it on his shoulder and got up.

'Are you going back now?' she asked.

'Yes, but I'll be here tomorrow at the same time.'

She was gazing at him.

'Come closer', she said.

He bent over the pillow. She pushed the sheet back and pulled his head down to her bosom.

'Someone might come in', he whispered.

'Let them', she whispered back.


Outside it was night. A spring night, perfumed with the warm smell of earth. He breathed deeply, carelessly, in the fresh cool air. After the close and excessively heated cubicle of the hospital the open night was very comforting. He looked at his watch. He would have time for a small beer before leaving for Prague, he thought with some satisfaction.

For some time she lay on her bed with her eyes closed. When she was sure he had left the hospital far behind she got up slowly. She opened the window. Outside, in the distance, the lights of a small town were twinkling. She was reminded of her room in the hostel at Prague. She had come away just two days ago, but it seemed an age had gone by. She stood at the window for some time. An infant was crying in the maternity ward. Soon there was complete silence.

She walked back to her bed. She took out an old towel from her suitcase. She rolled up the things he had brought for her in it, then walked back to the window and threw the bundle out into the darkness.

Her head was dizzy as she went back to her bed. The packet of cigarettes was still there on the stool.

She lit one, but it had a strange flavour. She crushed it against the floor and lay down. Her eyes were slightly wet, but she was soon sound asleep.

*Translated by Krishna Baldev Vaid*

# The Man and the Girl

As he pushed open the door of the bookshop a bell clanked once somewhere inside. He stepped in and the door slid to behind him. The bell now clanked twice.

The last clank reverberated through the close air—a lingering warning that someone had come in.

But there was no one within sight in the shop. It occurred to him that he might easily help himself to a few books and walk out unnoticed. Of course, this was no more than a stray thought, for he was aware that even as the bell went a pair of rheumy blue eyes, morose behind spectacles, clapped onto him from above the counter across the shop.

He made his way in through rows of bookcases.

'How do you do?' he said to the old manager behind the counter.

The manager shrugged his shoulders. The gesture gave no clue as to his mood.

'It's beginning to be cold,' he tried again. He had thought of the weather on seeing the moustache of the manager, which was as white as fresh snow.

'Yes,' the old man said indifferently, 'It's already October.'

'They haven't turned on the central heating yet.'

'It can't be before November, even if it snows.' The old man was given to sly digs at the government. He had been the owner of the bookshop until the new regime took it over with all its stock of books which his father—and *his* before him—had collected over the years since World War I. The shop still looked the same but the state had insinuated itself overnight, like the thin edge of the wedge, between him and his bequest. He continued to sit behind the counter but the relationship he now bore to the books resembled that of a father spying on his own children in an orphanage.

'Do you think it's going to snow?' the man asked.

The old man took off his glasses and wiped them with a handkerchief. Then he blew his nose. 'Death and snow do not ring the doorbell before breaking in,' he said at last.

It seemed to the man that the remark had been aimed at him. In the past whenever he had walked in the old man had been visibly annoyed. He said nothing but it was apparent from his manner that he —a foreigner—irritated him much the same way as the War, Hitler or communism had in the past.

He passed on ahead to the bookcases standing in the cold light of a grey day. He ran his eyes furtively all around but could not see the girl. Doubts assailed him: could it be that she had not come to the shop today at all? Shivering, he slipped his hand into his coat pocket. His fingers touched a telegram, and he pulled out his hand. There was no warmth in it, and none outside.

He stood about uncertainly in the middle of the shop, ill at ease under the old man's gaze. Then he took a couple of long steps and went round behind a bookcase. He dabbed a handkerchief to his forehead where cold sweat had broken out.

He heard a scraping sound behind him and turned at once. A trolley creaked along on its wheels on the other side. Then he saw the girl, pushing it with both hands on its handlebar, as if it were a pram, in which sat a pile of books where the child should have been.

The girl's head was bent over the trolley. She picked up the books one by one and put each in its place on the shelf. She peered through her glasses at each title and its author before dusting it and standing it in its row. She was so absorbed in her work that she was not aware of being watched from over the bookshelf.

He was watching her. An electric bulb from the ceiling overhead cast its light on her. She was a short-statured girl. She was wearing a long blue apron, like that of a working girl in any other shop, but it did not suit her: its indifferent folds enclosed almost the whole of her body. At the moment, nobody could have guessed that she was a twenty-year-old on whose last birthday a few days ago he had bought her flowers which might still be lying, although wilted, in her room.

Still unawares, the girl had edged along quite close to him across the bookcase. He could see her head though the space between the two upper shelves. Her dark brown hair, with a hesitant parting in the middle, was pulled back as usual and secured tightly at the nape of her neck.

He could no longer hold himself back. As the girl raised her hand to put the last of the books in its place, he reached out suddenly and laid his hand on hers on the cold metal sheet of the shelf. Startled, the girl almost screamed, sending him into a panic. Hurriedly, he pushed aside some books and thrust his head in: 'It's me,' he said.

The girl looked up at him wide-eyed, as if he were a djinn smiling among the books.

'Oh, it's you! When did you come in?'

'Just a little while ago . . . Were you scared?'

'Yes' the girl nodded. She did not lie even in trifling matters. Her hand still lay in the man's clasp. Her small breasts behind the apron rose and fell with her rapid breathing. She had indeed been frightened; he had never descended upon her quite like this ever before.

'Can you take some time off?'

'Now?' Her hand under his was cold.

'I'd like to have a moment with you alone,' he said.

'Why, is anything the matter?' the girl asked, her eyes widening again.

'No, no. Not for any particular reason,' he said, making light of it. While the girl never lied, he never spoke the truth directly.

'Go in. I'll be with you in a minute.'

She withdrew her hand from under his, looked up at him once, turned away, and disappeared behind the row of bookshelves.

A room at the back of the shop had been set apart for secondhand books. The girl would sit here on a stool. A curtain behind her partitioned off the room from the main shop and a tiny cabin, to which she retired during her lunch hour.

To this cabin, then, the man went. He had been

there a number of times in the past as well, and every time he had been seized with a particularly strong feeling that it was not a room off the main shop but her room in her own house. It was quiet in here: no voices or traffic noise penetrated to this place, except the rumble of a tram deep as the crash of thunder in a far-off corner of the city.

He lay back in a cane chair. The poorly ventilated room, dim from lack of daylight, smelt of old books. Mice could be heard scurrying somewhere along the walls. On a small three-legged table were kept tea things, slices of brown bread and soggy stale biscuits. The girl would withdraw to her cabin for a bite when hungry.

It was here that he had come upon the girl for the first time. He had come to sell off some of his old books. She was sitting behind the counter with her back to the door, nibbling at a slice of bread. An unfinished brown pullover stuck through with a pair of knitting needles lay on her lap. She gave a start when she heard him come in.

That was way back in March; now it was end-October. In these seven months he had sold off nearly all his old books—dictionaries, guide books, novels—which he did not want to take back home to his country. The girl bought the stuff for the shop and read it during her spare time. He was surprised to learn that she could not only read English but also speak it, though not so fluently.

In fact, it was this English which had broken the ice between the two. One day when going through the lot he had brought her, she had suddenly asked: 'Do the people of your country speak English?'

'No, it's not so,' he had said. 'I can't speak it well myself.'

'But you do,' she had insisted quite matter-of-factly before gathering the books in a pile in her arms. 'I'll be right back,' she had said and gone in behind the partition.

He had wondered then what books would finally be selected that day. They had a system of working, whereby the girl took the books to the manager who sorted out from the lot the ones he thought he could buy and returned the others. It was almost like gambling, for he was never sure what clinched the selection of a book. Once he had asked the girl about its mechanics but she ignored him. When he insisted—and this was much later on—she was annoyed: 'We keep only those books which we think are right for us.'

Fortunately, that day all his books except one— *Requiem For A Nun*—were found 'right'. While returning the book, the girl had looked at him curiously: 'Is this some sort of a religious book?'

'No,' he said, 'it's about a prostitute.'

He had wanted to shock her, because religion and prostitution—both these words—were taboo there. But no emotion showed itself on her face. However, she slipped the paperback onto the bottom shelf of the counter where she used to keep her lunchbox, napkin, key ring and other personal things.

He did not know how many of his books had, over these months, landed up on that shelf.

'It's a fat sum you've made today,' she said, running her eyes down the column of figures which a clicking adding machine had printed. He was tempted to steal a look at it but restrained himself. He would raise the balance somehow if this could fetch him even one-fourth of the rent due on his room.

'Can you tell how much it is?' she said, tearing off the slip from the machine. She put it down before him.

Forty crowns—he could hardly believe it! He had not been paid this much at one go ever before. The girl was smiling up at him, as if they had won a victory.

'So much?' he said.

'These are good days.'

Good days, surely! While in the bookshop her speech, her choice of words, shared with the Mohenjodaro script something of the latter's arcana: undeciphered, it held an aura of mystery; afterwards, it turned out to be so plain, obvious and run of the mill. Some nights when he could not get to sleep he could not help thinking of the girl and of some rag of a word or a lame sentence she had let drop: it floated— a bright object—through the darkness, clinging to the image of the girl. There were good days, bad days, and very bad days. The worst days were those when the girl returned all his books—regretfully, though: 'No luck today.' He would cram the lot into his duffel bag and walk out into the street. Even as he went away thinking about what books to take to her next which she, or the manager, might find worth buying, a shadow appeared behind the glass-panelled door of the shop. She watched him going away and wondered: 'What a man—he reads only English books.'

The manager saw it all, even while apparently dozing, telling himself that the man came over so often

not so much to dispose of the books as to meet the
girl. At his age! Imagine!

In a short while  the girl came to the cabin with her
lunch-box and stopped short in the doorway. The
man was sprawled over the chair, his eyes closed.
Fatigue lined his face, as if not only his past years but
even those yet ahead had chosen to take advantage of
his sleep to emerge on the pale skin across his cheek-
bones. The girl stared at him in silence. Had it been
some other day she would have been pleased at his
unexpected appearance in the shop, but today it
looked like it had the makings of a bad omen. She did
not believe in ghosts, but when he suddenly material-
ized before her across the bookshelf in his old overcoat with smudged collar sticking out on either side of
his neck like two dark wings, she was frightened out
of her wits: she stared at him in shock and disbelief, as
though a stranger were looking at her through his
familiar eyes. A stranger? She started across the
room, reaching out her hand to stroke him but checked herself in time, 'Let him have his nap,' she told
herself, 'there's lots of time yet.'

Usually, no client came in during the lunch-hour.

She opened her lunchbox. It contained a sandwich
made of salami between two slices of brown bread,
yoghurt in a small bottle, cheese cubes, and cucum-
ber soaked in vinegar. This was her everyday lunch.
Had she known that he was coming over she could
have brought an extra sandwich. She had, in fact,
told him on several occasions not to bother with
cooking in the morning and to share lunch with her at
the bookshop, but he had turned that down. He was

rather afraid of seeing her during daytime and kept away unless it could not be avoided. But what could it be that had made him come today? She had been with him just last night.

As she rose to put the kettle to boil she saw that he had woken and was watching her.

'Care for a nibble?' she asked.

He shook his head and straightened up in his chair. His eyes were shot with red. Shadowy traces of last night stuck to his shaved cheeks. He rubbed his eyes; a shred of a dream hovered momentarily in the stale air of the room before it dissolved and he saw the live girl in front of him.

The girl had, in the meantime, taken off her apron. She was wearing a green skirt which fell just short of her knees. Her girlish flesh peeped through her black stockings. A black belt gathered her dress at the waist like a schoolgirl's. A loose grey cardigan hung from her shoulders. The girl had an open look about her, unlike most other girls who wore a mask for the benefit of people at large.

The kettle had come to a boil. Steam hissed out in a jet from its spout. The girl poured it over coffee in two mugs. Beads of sweat glistened on her forehead.

'Are you coming from the apartment now?'

The man hesitated. His fingers closed round the telegram in his pocket.

'I'd gone to the Institute.'

'Have you finished the book?' This was the one question the girl never failed to ask him.

'No, not yet. I'd gone to ask for an advance.'

'How many pages are still left?'

'I've to do the last chapter now. But the manuscript has to be typed.'

'Can't the Institute even get it typed?' the girl said irritably.

'They have only one English typist and he is on leave.'

He began to stroke her arm gently. This was the only way they could overcome their anxieties. It carried them far beyond, although the girl stood still. She would be cold—particularly her feet. Whenever she came into his room the first thing that she did was to stretch out her legs by the fire side. It was surprising why, at her age, her hands and feet should be so cold.

'How soon have you to finish it?'

'In ten days. Fifteen, at the most.'

'Can I type it for you?'

'You?' The man smiled wanly.

'Why not? I can do it in the evenings'.

The girl had lately learnt to type in English. It came to be a game between the two of them. The man read out to her whatever he had translated and the girl let the English words leap out from under her fingers over the keyboard. Later, they went through the typed pages together to mark the typographical errors. The man believed that this way she could not only improve her typing but also her English. But the girl was not really keen on a crash programme of self-improvement; for her it was enough of a comfort just to be in the proximity of the man for those brief hours leased to them by the night when beyond the window stars shone in the sky like the letters on her keyboard . . . and as her fingers went tippity-tap on the keys the stars descended on the white foolscap paper.

The kettle was singing again. The girl switched it off and opened the window to let in a fresh draught.

'It's too hot,' she said, pouring another cup of coffee. As she leaned over the low table the chignon at the nape of her neck slid through an arc and came to rest on her shoulder. She seemed unaware of many little things like this which she did with her body. She would not have known how her fingertip sticky with her spit turned over the pages of the book and how her lips moved as she read. At such times he would watch her intently and wonder if she was the same girl whose body he had explored many a night but which appeared untouched by day. Even as he watched, he realized he was himself lying at the bottom of a pit, crouched like an animal, ready to leap out and pounce on the girl, wring her smooth neck and bolt out into the street away from the bookshop, from remorse, from sin . . . But when the girl raised her eyes to him, the violence that had been churning in the pit of his stomach dissolved and he returned her gaze. A smile broke out on the corners of her lips.

He leaned forward towards the girl and said, as if on the spur of the moment: 'I got a telegram late last night.'

'What telegram?' The cup in her hand hung in mid air.

'She has been taken ill and wants to see me.'

He took out the telegram from his pocket—a crumpled slip of red paper, a pitiable scrap. The girl turned away her eyes.

'What's the illness?' she asked calmly.

'I don't know. I'll have to find out.'

'When do you want to go?'

He merely stared at the telegram in silence.

'When are you leaving?' the girl asked again, a gentleness softening the edges of her casual tone.

'I think I'll wait for her letter.'

'But if she is really ill . . .' she trailed off.

'What do you mean? Do you think she is feigning illness?'

'No, I didn't mean that,' the girl said. 'I mean, if she is ill, you must hurry up.'

'Are *you* in a hurry?'

'I?'

'Yes—in a hurry to see me buzz off.'

The girl stared at him, her eyes wide with surprise and hurt. 'I don't understand,' she said.

'Why are you worried about her more than I am?'

He was being sarcastic. He had wished to go beyond sarcasm to where cruelty began. Instead, he had run into stark meanness and he stopped short. There was nothing around there except the dirt of weariness and regret. He had not slept a wink last night.

'I'd better go,' he said.

'Wait,' the girl said, putting out her hands on his knees. 'What did you say? Do you really think I am in a hurry?'

'I was only joking,' he said, squeezing her arm gently. The girl trembled all over.

'If I asked you not to go, would you listen to me?'

'But you never say anything.'

'It's because . . .' There seemed no point in going on. Whenever she had tried to put the man to the test, he had withdrawn into himself: he just wouldn't be there, and in his place she saw her sin which asked her the very questions she would ask the man. Sin had a way of entangling itself into knots with the passage of time.

'Is she often ill?' she asked. The girl preferred not to refer to his wife by her name but by the third person pronoun. She was glad she had never seen her.

The man gazed past the girl at the window behind her and the rooftops chequered by a thistledown sun. 'I had a dream last night,' he said.

'What was it?'

'I saw you looking up at my window from the street below. I called out to you but you had already turned round. I banged on the door with all my might. I wanted to rush down the stairs after you . . .'

'Really?'

'Then I woke up. There was actually someone out there knocking on the door. I thought you had returned. But it was the telegraph man.'

The man laughed, but the girl had a harried look about her. For her it added up to a foreboding. She lived among forebodings, and because of that liked to spend an hour or two in the church. She had not told the man about her visits to the church, not because she wanted to hide anything from him but because she thought faith in God was a kind of sickness—a very personal sickness—and she wanted to keep him away from it. A darkness surrounded God as it did his wife. She knew about his wife as little as he knew about her God—and both had better be left alone.

A shrill peal of the doorbell startled them and they

pulled away. She went to the door, slid the bolt and looked out. It was a customer. 'It's lunchtime,' she said. The man went away and she shut the door. But she did not turn round immediately; she stood by the closed door, looking through the glasspane at the day opening out in sunshine before her—a day in October emerging through the mist—while her mind went back to the time when she had not yet met the man and used to return home in the evening alone in a lonely city.

When finally she turned to face the man, a smile hovered on her lips.

'How far is it?' she asked.

'What is?' The man had got up to leave.

'The town where your wife lives.' She had actually used the word 'wife' in a manner that suggested she might be a friend of hers, after all.

The man seemed to be in a haste. 'It takes about an hour,' he said.

'How would you go?'

'By bus, of course. You can get one every hour or so.'

The girl went over to him and looked up into his eyes. 'Can I come with you?'

'You?'

'I'd like to see you off at the bus station.'

The man stared at the girl for a stupefied moment while silence gathered about her, swept over the telegram, and lapped against the rows of books that contained all the secrets of life—or of death—but which offered no solace then, no help, either to her or to him.

He picked his duffel bag and came up close against

the girl and lowered his lips to her small head. She
looked small, like a helpless schoolgirl. It struck him
then that the forty years of his age were flowing like a
muddy stream through the shop, too shallow to
drown in but still deep enough to drag the girl after
him into its filth.

He walked out.

The girl ran to the window. The man was crossing
the street. She looked on as he grew small in the distance.

The next evening the girl strolled over to the man's
apartment, although she knew that he could not have
returned so soon. He had gone away to see his wife
late the previous afternoon. The girl had a duplicate
key to the apartment so that she could walk in any
time it pleased her.

There was, of course, no one in the apartment. The
stairs lay under darkness. Even the concierge had
gone out. She did not feel like going in; instead, she
backed out across the street for a better view of the
man's room on the third floor. It had a window
which looked out on a park.

Children were playing in the park.

And the window was closed. The man had forgotten to drop the curtain in place before leaving. The
sun slanted into the windowpanes and one could see
inside. There was the typewriter on a table, a shirt on
the wall, a vase—which she had bought for him—on
the window-sill . . . On an impulse she decided to
go in. She reached into her bag for the key but the
persistent thought at the back of her mind that he was
not there trickled down to her fingertips. She turned

back towards the park and walked slowly away on the grass.

There was a duck-pond in the middle of the park.

Preoccupied with her thoughts she walked on by the pond. Her brain fumbled for the elusive string which she could pull to unravel her gnarled emotions. All her thoughts began with the man. It was a day as usual when he had walked into the bookshop for the first time. Little did she realize then that before long she herself would be embroiled with him in an unusual affair. After he had left his books on the counter she would turn over the pages, some brittle with age, out of curiosity, and come upon, on the fly-leaf, his name over the name of his city and the date on which the book had been bought . . . and she would be wonderstruck to think that she had not even been born when some of those books were acquired by him . . . that she was at school when he was already grown up, went to college and, later, married. People in the street took her for his daughter. She smiled to herself; this must be the reason, she thought, why he fought shy of being seen with her during the day. As far as she was concerned, she was not bothered by his age, or her own, or the years between them. What was the point? Age was like so much snowfall during the night while one slept: one didn't even know it had snowed until one woke up in the morning and found heaps of it at the doorstep.

Thinking about snow, the girl recalled that other night, their first night together in his bed, way back in March. That night they had the last snowfall of the season. Icy gusts sent shivers through the city. She was numb with cold when she came out. The man had tried to dissuade her but an unsuspected fire within her that could have consumed the entire city, as it were, urged her on. She walked the streets until her feet refused to carry her any further. At last she found herself in a familiar old church deserted at that hour.

She made her way along the dark aisle to the front pew. Just a little while ago she had been lying with the man in his bed. Now she was sitting in the front pew in a church. What did she think she was doing here? Through befuddled eyes she saw a man above the altar, pierced through his wrists and ankles with nails: what could *he* be doing there? Suddenly, then, she realized she was not alone. There was someone beside her on the pew she had not seen before in the darkness. It was an old woman, swaying like the flame of candle in a draught and mumbling a prayer. She was taken aback to see that one could, even at the fag end of a long life, when the game was already up, still have some favour or the other to ask of the Lord. She slid closer to the woman. 'Listen,' she whispered in her ear, 'Is it a sin to sleep with a man whose wife is still alive?'

'Who? Who is alive?' The woman looked the girl in her face.

The next moment the woman started laughing. From her toothless cavernous mouth gushed a blast charged with alcohol. Her ravaged tear-stained cheeks worked involuntarily.

The girl could not stand it and ran out. The old woman's face pursued her in the streets until it stopped snowing and her mind went blank from exhaus-

tion. It was March then—and the first time she had
slept with the man.

Seven months later she was sitting in the park in
front of his apartment house. The children had left
long ago. The ducks too had disappeared. The darkness had spilled all over without a splash or a sound.
The lights in the houses around had been turned on.
Only his room on the third floor was unlit—a dark
empty shell. There was nothing there now—neither
the vase, nor the table, nor the shirt hanging on the
wall.

He was not there. He was in another town—with
his wife. Not sleeping, in fact—nor awake—but
thinking of the day he had first run into the girl in the
bookshop. That was seven months ago, and now his
wife was breathing heavily beside him.

He returned after three days—the interregnum divided by two long nights into three short workdays,
while the girl tramped to and back from the bookshop as usual. Once, in the evening, she had gone to
the bus station, although she did not know when he
was to get back. Another evening she had spent in the
park watching the children and the ducks. The man,
of course, must have been visiting his wife now and
then—but for the girl this was, in her short life, the
first and therefore mysterious encounter with what
was a non-thing. How could one's not being around
be a thing in itself? Yet, it walked with her in the
streets, lay down beside her in her bed at night, and
kept awake watching her fall asleep . . . And then it
dawned on her why men, lonely and alone, went to
the church, or to pubs, or into those houses where

women traded their flesh—or, if married, went to
their wives despite the fact that their happiness in
each other had long since vanished.

But the girl was not bothered about happiness; she
would rather not give it a second thought. All that
she wanted to know was if he knew what it was that
he had left behind with her when he went away. Did
he know what accompanied her like her own shadow? Perhaps he did. This could be the reason why at
times he seemed to be struggling to keep away from
her, and since he could not really keep his resolve he
was often tense and edgy and abrupt with her—just
like he had been on the telephone today, his voice a
snappish croak.

He had rung her up on the third day during
the lunch-hour when the manager was out. She was
in her cabin, laying out the lunch. When the telephone tinkled she had a container in her hands. 'It's
him,' she thought—although the telephone rings
much the same way for everyone—and rushed past the
bookcases to the counter and picked up the receiver.
She listened to his voice, and as she returned to her
cabin she looked out at the tree in the window, the
street below, and a bill posted on the wall opposite. A
corner of the bill had come unstuck and fluttered in
the wind.

His voice coming through the phone had sunk
deep in her. It rose now through a mild unhappiness
and resentment. Why did he have to be in high
dudgeon? He hadn't even asked what she'd done
these three days. All this while he had been away
with his wife—and now, to take it out on her! Was he
crazy?

She stuffed a bag with the underground books which could not be sold over the counter. She had acquired them, paying for them with her own money, from a godown where books of that sort were usually stashed away to rot.

Even as she put away the books in the bag one after another she could see the man in his room, alone on this cold and dull day, his typewriter on the table littered with foolscap sheets the way he had left it before going away.

He was squatting on his heels, trying to light a fire. He thrust old papers under the fire-grate. Smoke swirled up and around in the chimney. He choked on it and his eyes watered. He rubbed his eyes dry on his elbow.

The girl was lying on the couch, a cushion under her head. Beneath it her lunchbox lay on top of the bag full of books on the floor. It smelt of salami and sourish stale yoghurt. Her eyes were open, her head was turned, and she was looking at the back of the man—at the shirt-tail hanging out of his trousers.

Flames burst out as the man finally turned his head sideways. The girl—across the smoke and the flames—swam in his tearful eyes. He got up and went over to her. He sat down by her head which rested on a cushion, while her feet dangled over the edge of the couch. He recalled how the girl's feet in her nylon stockings were always cold. She was so still that the slight movement of her feet seemed illusory. 'Are you cold?' he asked her.

The girl's feet froze. 'No,' she said, shaking her head.

'It was very cold in the bus. The water by the road-side had frozen.'

'When did you get back?'

'Around lunchtime. I rang you as soon as I got back.'

'What was the illness?'

'Nothing in particular,' he said.

'Nothing at all?'

'She wanted to see me.' The man passed his hand over his face, as if smoothing out the wrinkles there.

'And it took her three days?'

'What?'

'It took her all of three days to see you?'

The man raised his head and gazed at her in bewilderment. Her face was flushed with more than the heat of the crackling fire in the room. She had a strange pleading look in her eyes. The man took her hand. He stroked it gently—a small white hand that had so far known only the touch of second-hand books but had not yet grasped what was written on their brittle pages, wherein people married, separated, aged, and died alone in their rooms. An intense warmth that had nothing to do with desire surged through him. He gathered her in his arms under the spread of his full forty years and she came readily, snuggling up against his chest like a dove.

'Did you sleep with her?' The girl's voice was so faint he was not sure he wasn't hallucinating.

'What did you say?'

'Did you . . . ?'

The man raised his head. He let his hands cup about her face and ever so gently tipped it upwards. She looked up into his face lined by tiredness and sleep and age, and in a vivid instant realized she loved him, that whatever he might have to say about what she had asked him did not matter either way.

The live coals in the fireplace glowed to suffuse the room with warm brightness.

In a moment the girl rose from the couch and sat down at the study table. She looked at the sheet inserted in the typewriter—and let her eyes glide past towards the window. Darkness had settled over the park. The duck pond, by contrast, showed through like a whitish stretch. The streetlights were strung out in an enormous festoon across the city . . . . She pulled her chair closer to the table and began to type slowly, hesitantly, the story that the man had translated in longhand. As her fingers moved over the keys, a tranquillity descended on her; she felt free to roam at will, free from danger while the man watched her from the couch, in the lush forest that mushroomed in the space between the two languages.

The man looked at the girl's head bent over the typewriter. Her blond chignon hung rather low and loose to one side of her neck. Her mouth formed the words as she read and even as the words fluttered about over her lips she collected them together on the sheet in the typewriter. She had by now forgotten all about his wife. She didn't even let his presence intrude on her. Occasionally, though, she turned in his direction to ask him the meaning of a word or two. The man, as he looked on, thought to himself that yesterday night he was with his wife, tomorrow he would go to the bookshop again, and in a few days he would go to his wife before returning to this room, to this girl again . . . and again . . . and again: what was the meaning, if any, in the recurring pattern of his days?

He stretched out his hand and touched the girl between her shoulders. She started at his touch and turned round. A faint smile appeared on her pale lips.

'Is there anything you want?'

'Leave it now. You can do the rest of it tomorrow.'

'There is very little left to do. Why don't you go to sleep?'

And the man wondered to himself how it was that a girl could turn into a mother without passing through the stage of becoming a wife and bearing a child. He closed his eyes. In the darkness behind his eyelids the typewriter pounded out only one word over and again: sleep, sleep, sleep . . . But there was no sleep anywhere.

The girl went on typing slowly late into the night until she reached the end of the chapter. When she was lost in the dark forested mazes of the story she let either the man or the dictionary take her hand and guide her into the bright glow of meaning, from where she could carry on on her own. Slowly, then, she arrived at the end and paused on the black dot of the full stop on the white sheet. She stared at the portion of the sheet left blank and empty like the three days she was alone on the streets while he was away, and then it struck her that emptiness was a word whose meaning she could neither ask the man nor look up in the dictionary.

She pulled out the page, shut up the typewriter in its case, pushed back her chair, and came to stand in the middle of the room. The bag of books lay on the floor. The man had stretched out on the couch on one side. She thought that if she decided to walk out then, down the stairs and away into the street, no one would be any the wiser.

Then her attention wandered off. She saw a trapped moth beat its wings against the windowpane, buzzing up and down along it in desperation. She threw open the window and the moth escaped into the darkness with its tiny little life, brushing the cheek of the girl. She stared after it, trying to penetrate the darkness below.

A red neon sign atop a bar shone fuzzily through the October mist. A man pickled to the gills emerged from the bar and weaved unsteadily across the street in the manner of the moth on the windowpane. Suddenly he turned and sidled up against the wall right below the window where the girl stood looking out, and unfastened his fly. The girl shut the window at once and turned back into the room. She removed her hairpins, undid her chignon and let her hair fall about her shoulders. She took out a vaseline tube from her bag, squeezed it on her fingertip, and rubbed it lightly on her face, behind her ears and on her arms. As she did it, it occurred to her that *she* too might have done all this before going to him at night. She held her hand at the thought, while something heaved within her, writhing all over. She had not known of it before—this unclean slimy pain, like a restless worm turning and rearing its head for all it was worth to crawl up and out to seek its escape. Instead, it burrowed deeper in her, and terror gripped her. It stuck like a lump of ash in her throat. She put a hand over her mouth and fled to the bathroom. She doubled over the basin and threw up what had been throwing its weight about inside her—yellow curdled flakes floating in water.

The girl washed herself after vomiting, splashed water into her eyes and reached out for a towel. As she straightened up with the towel in her hands, she glanced in the mirror above the basin. Peeping out of it she saw an old woman with a face crumbling, hollow-cheeked and toothless—the one she had run across in the church seven months ago—but she was not laughing now, she was looking on at her sadly. She had apparently something to say to the girl, but the girl was not ready to listen: she would rather not be told about her sin—neither past, nor that which still lay ahead. Before the old woman could open her mouth the girl turned on her heels and left her alone in the mirror.

She was back in the room. She drew up to the man on the couch. She turned off the light but it did not plunge the room into darkness: the remains of the fire cast a glow on the typewriter, her bag of books, his head on the cushion . . . She slipped out of her clothes, took a blanket from the cabinet, tucked it round the man and then slipped under it herself beside him.

He was lying so still that she could not make out whether he had woken up or was asleep. Only his breathing could be heard—a grinding rumble in his chest. Her groping fingers touched him on his chest where his open shirt had pulled away—where a few white hairs grew, and she let her head rest on it. The man shivered in his sleep. A warm surge thudded along in his blood. 'No, no,' a voice within him spoke to him; but, awake, he saw the top of the girl's

head on his chest, her unbound tousled hair yet
another darkness in the dark room. Her shoulders
shook, but it was some time before he realized that
she was crying and that a warm runnel coursed
through the clump of hairs on his chest.

'*Suno*,' the man spoke to her in his mother tongue,
'*I want to die*.'

The girl turned her face toward him uncomprehen-
dingly. Sometimes the man did lapse into the language of his country which she did not understand at
all.

'What did you say?'

His hand stroked her small head gently, ever so
gently, soothingly. She was no longer the woman
who had mothered him only a short while ago but a
mere girl again and he had spoken to her a truth that
she could not have translated.

*Translated by Kuldip Singh*

# A Room of Their Own

They walked with long steps as if they were being pursued. When the girl was out of breath the boy took her hand and gave it a little squeeze. Their eyes met for a moment before they resumed walking.

'Do you want to sit down somewhere for a while?' he asked her uncertainly.

'Where?' Her interest mildly aroused, she looked around, evincing curiosity more than hope.

'I know a spot. It's not far away.'

She slipped her hand into his. The pavement gleamed under the streetlights. Secretly she began to count every other flagstone, for it pleased her very much if the street came to an end on an even number.

There couldn't have been any street or lane in the city they had not tramped together. They roamed all over not because they liked walking but because it was the only way they could be with each other. They did not have a room of their own. The boy was putting up in a hostel where he had to share his room with five other boys. He could never gather enough courage to take the girl there. The girl did have a room to herself but it was in the precincts of a religious order where men were not allowed.

But it was a large city and they had learnt to live on

the streets, as it were. When tired out they sneaked into a dark passageway by the stairs of some house. No one disturbed them there. It was in the seclusion of such a shelter that the boy had kissed her for the first time; her coat was stained white where it brushed against the lime wash on the wall. The stairs provided them with some measure of relief from the coldness of the streets.

It wasn't too cold that day: the winter was drawing to an end. Light fluffy clouds drifted overhead. The snow melting on the cornices dripped onto their shoulders or hair as they wandered through the streets close to the houses or shops.

They would stop now and then in front of a brightly lit show-window.

'Do you like it?' the girl asked good-humouredly, pointing to a cut-glass vase. The boy looked up at her, but before he could speak the girl moved on to another show-window: it was something of a game between the two.

While thus window-shopping they would put on a mask of joviality and banter, although to them the show-windows were rather mysterious because they gave on to something lasting, warm and frail—protected from the corrosion of the wayside dust and the understairs darkness of other people's houses. Every shop was almost half of home. To linger in front of its show-window was not merely to pass the time but to dream about a childhood lost to a hostel or rented room.

'Do you like this?' the girl asked him, eyeing the rich curtain cloth displayed in another show-window. But the boy was looking elsewhere.

'How do you like this?' the girl asked again, pointing out the cloth to him. Her gaze was still fastened on it.

'It's rather darkish', the boy said shyly.

'But it should go with a deep-red rug—won't it?'

The boy did not answer her. The sight of the rug had transported him to a half-forgotten room. There used to be a piano by the window and on it the family album with vines along its margin. He smiled to himself.

'What are you thinking about?' The girl found his preoccupied smile rather annoying.

'I think I've seen curtains like this one before. It was a large room with yellow flowers on the wallpaper.'

The girl was struck with a feeling of wonder. She could never think quite like the boy. What he had said had instantly emptied the room for her of all its things excepting the yellow flowered wallpaper bathed with a liquid light. And for this she loved him all the more. He was never stuck on anything like her. He could see immediately beyond what was at hand, relate it with another experience diverse in itself and create out of this juxtaposition something new and startlingly familiar.

They had moved on to a bridge across the river which ran through the heart of the city and were now standing close to the railing, watching some birds flutter around in the fading light above the river.

'Some rooms are always full of flowers', the girl remarked. She was still thinking about the wallpaper. She wanted their conversation to proceed along a trodden and predictable path.

But the boy was given to straying. 'The last time I saw a heap of flowers in a room was when my grand-mother died.'

'Was she very old?'

'I don't know. I don't remember ever having seen her before. She used to live in another city.'

'Oh.'

'She looked like a doll amid all those flowers.'

The girl watched in silence the birds fly low above the river. 'I've never seen a dead person', she told herself thoughtfully.

There were a number of bridges over the river as it meandered through the middle of the city. Some-times while crossing a bridge one had a feeling one was leaving not just half the city behind but all of it, and going into another city ahead. The bridge they were walking on was the oldest. Along either side of it stood ancient statues of Christian saints. An approach-ing tram cast shadows of the saints on the water and the shadows skipped across as the tram clanked by.

She held on to the boy's arm as they went down the bridge. Bridges scared her. Often she had a pecul-iar feeling, as if she were walking on water and that she would be sucked deep down into it the moment she let go of the boy. It was a giddying thought.

'How long can you walk still?' the girl asked.

'I could still walk a long distance if I didn't have to go back to the hostel.' The boy let his head drop on her shoulder. She ran her fingers through his hair playfully. Earlier when they happened to touch each other by chance, it used to make them very happy; of late they touched each other when very happy, and it made them sad.

'Do you think you'd like us to walk even when we'd a room to ourselves?' Her fingers slid through his hair and stopped short on his face.

The boy had never really thought in that way. When alone in his room he often dreamt of places where the two of them could be by themselves. Sometimes he prayed that his roommates would discreetly spend a night elsewhere and leave the room to him and the girl till the dawn; but his prayer was never answered.

They walked past a row of houses where the poor lived. Clothes-lines had been strung across the walls and sagged under limp wet washing. The houses enclosed an open space used by the children as a playground. Their shouts overflowed into the neighbouring lanes. Chimneys stuck out above the roofs, black against a darkening sky.

'Where are we going?' the girl asked.

'There's a movie theatre close by.'

'You want to see a movie?'

'It wouldn't be cold inside.'

'Are you cold now?'

'No, no', the boy said hurriedly. He put his hand on her shoulder. 'You know, I don't really feel anything of the sort when I'm with you.'

'You feel nothing, is it?' the girl said, feigning disappointment.

The boy flushed. He was one of those who could not say the right thing in the right manner at the right moment. He talked of something either in the far future, which baffled the girl, or in the far past, which left the girl depressed. She for her part wished she could take advantage of the boy's weakness—but it would have made neither of them happy. Since they had very little time together they both watched their every step carefully. Those who do not or cannot live together rarely toy with each other's happiness; on the contrary they guard it zealously.

Leaving the square behind they entered a narrow lane with only a few shops in it. They were now in the outskirts of the city. The neon light over a lone pub went on and off. Crowded together in this lane were an old cinema, a petrol station, two dance halls and, furthest out, an abandoned bus terminus. Street-lights stopped here.

The woman at the box-office had dozed off. She had not been expecting anyone to turn up and so was annoyed to see them. A suburban cinema hall, it showed only those films which had had a prolonged run of several months at the downtown theatres.

'Wait a second,' the boy said, dipping into the in-side pocket of his coat: 'Let me get the tickets.' But the girl did not wait for him for she knew his scholarship allowance was much less than her own pay packet. She worked at restoring valuable old paint-ings in a museum and the boy often called her, in jest, Miss Restorer.

The girl took out a crumpled note from her hand-bag and bought the tickets. Meanwhile the boy ling-ered over in front of the stills from the film. Occa-sions such as this were quite embarrassing to him but he would not protest, for that might make it worse still for him—and for the girl too.

The picture had started already. There were very few people in the hall; almost all the back rows were empty. The woman who ushered them in did not even bother to switch on her flashlight and show them to their seats; she told them to sit anywhere they wanted. They found themselves seats in one of the back rows. A cinema hall was the only other place besides the dark passageways which offered them some privacy.

The boy turned in his chair and gently kissed the girl. Then he let his hand stray to the edge of her skirt at the knee. Some way up the thigh was her sock suspender. . . The girl quietly held his prying hand back and pulled the skirt low over her knees.

They turned their eyes to the screen. It was an old Italian film called *La Strada* and it was dubbed. They read the accompanying captions for some time before the girl got bored. 'Will you please read it aloud for me?' she said to the boy.

The boy began to read out the captions to her in whispers. But he would hardly read half the caption before it was replaced by another. They appeared in such rapid succession that before long he despaired and fell silent.

The girl had dozed off, but as soon as the boy stopped reading she woke up with a hint of reproach in her eyes and asked him to go on reading to her; she was listening all right, she said; and when the boy resumed reading she promptly fell asleep again. Her head sank and came to rest on his shoulder. Her mouth was slightly open and she mumbled in her sleep. The boy tried to make out her words but mostly failed. He then turned his attention back to the mad heroine of *La Strada* on the screen.

When the movie was over he gently removed the girl's head from his shoulder. 'Look', he called out to her softly, 'let's go out.'

The girl blinked her eyes against the hall lights. An apologetic smile hovered at the corners of her lips.

They went out. The girl was feeling refreshed after her nap; the knots of fatigue had come undone inside her.

'I dropped off to sleep', the girl said, doing her hair. 'Whatever happened to that mad woman in the end?'

'She wasn't mad. She only looked like one.'

'She had a strange way of laughing.'

'Oh yes.' The boy had never before seen anyone laugh in such a weird manner. It reminded him of everything normal people lose sight of when growing up. But this woman had lost nothing and therefore was herself lost and very nearly mad.

'Listen.' She took the boy's hand. 'I want an icecream.'

There was a buffet bar nextdoor to the cinema. He got a gimlet for himself and an icecream for her. This time the girl did not offer to pay: she would let the boy spend occasionally.

Outside the darkness seemed to have mellowed; a sort of pale luminescence, left behind in the wake of the winter, permeated it. Streetlights downtown obscured it, but in the open suburban sky it diffused its soft glow through the dark layers of the air.

They stopped by the traffic lights at the intersection where the road from the city split into several offshoots Surmounting the traffic lights was a signpost with a number of arrowheads which pointed into different directions and bore the names of different cities—Berlin, Paris, Nuremberg, Dresden. . . . The names shone in the light. Standing here one felt one was right in the middle of Europe.

'Just have a look,' the boy said to the girl. 'See how many cities there are!'

The girl's eyes were wide with amazement and a lurking fear—which only those who are still young can have for they have an entire life still ahead of them—like the fear one feels when holding some very frail and precious article in one's hand: the pleasure of its touch is less than the fear of dropping it.

'Which of the cities would you like to go to?' the boy asked jokingly.

'Dresden, then Leipzig, and. . .'

'And?'

The girl was lost in thought. This was yet another game, besides window-shopping, they fancied: they often found themselves talking about cities neither of them had ever visited. Not that they had not been out: they had in fact been to several cities—the girl as a child with her parents and the boy by himself a few years ago. But they had never been to any city together and so they dreamt about being together in Rome or Paris, albeit in a cheap hotel. They desired neither Rome nor Paris for the sights there, but only for what these promised by way of a room in a hotel, with perhaps an attached bath. After gadding about the city all day long she would take a leisurely shower while the boy waited for her in the adjoining room. After the bath she would make her bed while the boy made his, knowing full well they would need only one of the beds. This was happiness, the greatest, the most unbelievable, the most miraculous. . . But she stopped herself short. One must never think of future happiness so vividly, she told herself, for that des-

troys it. This was one of her superstitions but she believed earnestly that happiness never came alive the
way one thought about it.

'Look, you're spoiling your icecream.'

She was still staring at the arrowheads above the
traffic lights.

They started walking in the direction of the city.
They could see the lights over the dam in the distance. The river glimmered with the misted puddles
of light. They were back on the bridge where the
thought of death had come to the girl earlier in the
evening. The statues of the saints were concealed by
the dark. Tramlight wavered on their heads, bent
perpetually in prayer.

'Where do we meet tomorrow?' the boy asked.
'Opposite the museum, isn't it?'

'Yes, I'll be there. But you know tomorrow is a
hot-water day. I'd like to go straight home—I haven't
had a bath in a month.'

The boy walked in silence beside her. He hated
hot-water days for on such days he had to spend his
evenings alone in his cramped hostel room.

'But you can come to the museum. We'll walk to
my room together', the girl said reassuringly.

They were back again at the row of cheap houses in
the poor locality. The last of the groups of boys and
girls lingered outside the pub and the cafe. The air
carried coal dust, the smell of drying clothes and
familiar household odours. Occasionally a small girl
would go running across or along the street to her
house with a frothy mug of beer.

They emerged onto a deserted lane. There was no
pub here, only rows of stolid old residential houses

that had stood there since well past the turn of the century. There was a solitary streetlight which cast its glow on an alert cat. The cat looked sideways before it bolted across the lane.

The girl halted abruptly, looking up at an upper-storey room. Two or three shadows floated across the curtain and disappeared into the house.

'What's up?' the boy asked impatiently.

'Can't you see?' the girl said quietly, turning her gaze back to the window. It was a narrow lane. The aerial poles reached out into the darkness above the roofs and a kite entangled there fluttered in the breeze.

An old woman leaned out of the window. Her hair looked like fluffed-up cotton in the electric light. In the part of the room behind her the wall was hung with pictures, and against it stood a bookcase, a piano and a vase.

They stood still. The girl shivered in the cold.

'She is looking at us,' the boy whispered.

The girl clasped his hand the more firmly out of sudden fright. 'Let's go on', she muttered urgently.

But the boy did not stir; he stood rooted as if hypnotized; and his eyes engulfed the room, its curtains, the wall with a picture-frame nailed to it and a conical shadow alongside, and the vase on the piano.

The woman was looking at them. In her weary, faded eyes there welled a tenderness—more than that it was a reflection of some unfulfilled longing which, wrung out of her, stood beside her, pale and wan. She looked at them standing out in the cold darkness without moving her eyes. Even as they returned her gaze a tiny distracted smile, perhaps unrelated to either her home or anything in it, flickered on her lips and in her dreamy eyes. This disturbed the boy and the girl. They were puzzled: was she looking at them or beyond into the darkness for what she had lost years ago.

'Come on now!' The girl tugged at his arm as a cold shiver ran down her spine.

They walked away with long strides. Their footsteps resounded in their ears as they hurried along.

After a while the girl broke the silence: 'Do you think the woman could see us in the dark?'

The boy thought about this for a long moment. 'No, she couldn't have', he said finally.

'Did you see the flowers in the room?'

The boy walked on in silence. Yes he had seen the flowers. Some rooms were always full of flowers, he reminded himself. His grandmother had died in her own room and had looked like a doll with all those flowers about her.

They passed by the show-windows which still splashed bright light across the pavement. Neon lights blinked merrily up the street. And the sky above the diffuse glow was unfolded into a huge dark awning.

Surprisingly it seemed a relief to know they didn't have a room of their own. They were almost glad, for the first time that evening, to be out in the street.

*Translated by Kuldip Singh*